Toyotomi
HIDEYOSHI
The Making of a Modern Hero

KATRICE CHANHSAMONE

Paperback: 978-1-966652-25-0
Hardcover: 978-1-966652-91-5
eBook: 978-1-966652-26-7
Library of Congress Control Number: 2025900860

Ordering Information:

Prime Seven Media
518 Landmann St.
Tomah City, WI 54660

Printed in the United States of America

ACKNOWLEDGEMENTS

The summer grasses
Of brave soldiers' dreams
The aftermath

Natsugusa ya
Tsuwamono domo ga
Yume no ato

— Matsuo Basho

Dedicated to Megumi Tachikawa.
Your inspiration and enthusiasm captivated
and guided my own beyond belief.
I am truly grateful.

Special thanks to
those whose constant support never failed me;
Judith Snodgrass, Koji Shiga, Amu Hosaka,
Akira Iwai and Hiroshi Nagata.

For Mum and Dad and my two young samurais
Paxton and Phoenix.

CONTENTS

ABSTRACT

Oda Nobunaga, Toyotomi Hideyoshi and Tokugawa Ieyasu were the three most powerful warlords of the sixteenth and early seventeenth century who successfully created a unified Japanese state by bringing to an end the civil wars.

For this, they would go down in history as 'the unifiers'. Although the unification was achieved through the accumulated efforts of the three, Hideyoshi has emerged as the most popular among contemporary representations. Perhaps because of his brilliance in 'making himself' a democratic ideal, and consequently bringing to completion the unification of the warring states of feudal Japan, holds a special place in the hearts of modern Japanese.

It is for this reason that I propose to study the presence of Hideyoshi in contemporary society, examining the factors behind the way he is 'promoted' in the story of his rise from a humble monkey-faced boy of peasant origins to that of a magnificent general and skilled unifier. In examining how Hideyoshi became 'heroized', I reveal how he is represented as such in the modern world, discussing his importance in today's Japan by looking at what remains of his legacy and why ultimately this sixteenth century warlord is exalted in modern social memory.

MAPS AND ILLUSTRATIONS

INTRODUCTION

In the sixteenth and early seventeenth centuries, Oda Nobunaga, Toyotomi Hideyoshi and Tokugawa Ieyasu successfully created a unified Japanese state by bringing to an end the civil wars. The most ingenious man of those three 'unifiers' was Toyotomi Hideyoshi. Although primarily this examination will focus on Hideyoshi as a 'conquering hero', the efforts and influence that the other unifiers had on Hideyoshi's life and society in the latter half of sixteenth century Japan will not go entirely unnoticed. I explore the important events and changes that occurred in medieval Japan at a time when Nobunaga and Hideyoshi successively were establishing the early modern Japanese state.

In examining how Hideyoshi became 'heroized', I venture to show how he is represented as such in modern Japan through various sources, ceremonies, shrines and in memory. Similarly, I can compare my observations to representations of Hideyoshi's predecessor, Nobunaga, and successor, Ieyasu amidst the furor of traversing into the twenty first century. I will look at a wide range of sources, both English and Japanese, including my own interpretation of the national TV channel NHK's portrayal of the very popular *Hideyoshi*, a widely watched mini-series drama, which ran consecutively for twelve weeks on Japanese prime time TV in 1996.

Living in Japan throughout my twenties gave me the opportunity to collect journal articles, *manga* (Japanese comics), commemorative literature, educational materials such as history school textbooks, and also the chance to conduct public surveys and discussions relevant to this topic. Different opinions about Hideyoshi and his rule, during a time when the samurai still reigned supreme over military and administrative authority, vary greatly between gender and generation in today's Japan.

Closely related to the once samurai ideal, modern Japan is as well- known for order and harmony as it is for a keen sense of personal honor. Under the dictator Toyotomi Hideyoshi, samurai power reached its most ostentatious development. Balancing progress in civility by continued practice of the military arts, the samurai engaged heavily in national and local administration—simply because they were understood by the rest of Japanese society as those who had the power to resolve conflicts and keep the peace. Himself a samurai and successful military leader and administrator, Hideyoshi also brought his power onto the social prestige of the high nobility, eventually legitimating himself through the title of *kampaku* or Imperial Regent. Just over four hundred and fifty years earlier, at the height of samurai power amidst the chaos and uncertainty of civil war, the populace of medieval Japan lived under the samurai regime. For more than seven centuries Japan was dominated by this military caste. Today, it still greatly influences social morals and spirit. Therefore, it is necessary to some degree to study and understand the actions of the samurai, as it is from this position that Hideyoshi ultimately succeeded in winning the *tenka* (the realm) and thereby serving as its ruling authority.

This book is divided into three parts. Part 1 looks at how Hideyoshi 'rose' from obscure beginnings and legitimated himself to the court (the emperor) in order to gain authority on a much greater level.

Part 2 investigates the means of his court legitimation and his power by focusing on his stronghold, Osaka Castle. Hideyoshi 'the warrior' used its magnificence to acquire the attitudes and prestige of the court nobility.

Part 3 examines Toyotomi Hideyoshi into the twenty first century by looking at his portrayal in the 1996 NHK TV drama and presence in other literary material, such as in school textbooks and *manga*. In conclusion, his importance, in a now very technological Japan, explores what remains of his legacy and why ultimately he became a necessary 'hero' in the permanent memory of society.

JAPAN
IN THE
AZUCHI-MOMOYAMA PERIOD
安土桃山時代の日本

Land of the Oda clan, 1560

Area conquered by Oda Nobunaga and Toyotomi Hideyoshi by 1582

Main Daimyō opposed to Hideyoshi in 1582

Other areas

● Castle town

○ Town

× Battle

Ukita Daimyō house

Hokkaidō

● Hirosaki   ● Hachinohe

● Akita   ● Morioka

● Ichinoseki

● Tsuruoka

Sea of Japan

Sado

● Sendai
● Shibata Yamagata
○ Niigata
● Nagaoka   ● Aizu
○ Takata   ● Shirakawa
Uesugi   ● Iwaki

Korea

Oki

Kanazawa ● Toyama   Takeda *Honshū*
● Sasa
Takasaki   ● Utsunomiya
● Fukui   Maeda

Shibata
Hojo
Edo ●
Matsue   ● Tottori   ● Iida   Odawara   ○ Choshi
Yonago   ● Obama   Akechi   × *Sekigahara* (1600)
Ukita   Kyoto○ Azuchi   Nagoya   × *Odawara* (1590)
Hamada   Himeji   ● Momoyama   Tokugawa
Mori   Okayama   ● Kobe   Yoshida
● Hagi   Hiroshima   ○ Osaka   ● Toba
○ Sakai

Tsushima   *Izu Islands*

Inland Sea   ● Takamatsu

● Kitakyushu   ● Matsuyama   ● Tokushima
○ Hakataka   Chosokabe   ● Kochi   ● Tanabe
● Hirado   Kobayakawa   Funai ●   ● Uwajima   *Shikoku*
○ Hara   ● Higo   Otomo
Fukue   Nagasaki ○
Kyūshū

PACIFIC OCEAN

Shimazu   ● Miyazaki
Kagoshima ●

East China Sea

Tanegashima

Yakushima

0   100   200 km

Map of Sixteenth Century Central Japan

XV

HIDEYOSHI AND FOUCAULT: GENEALOGY, TRUTH AND POWER

According to Michel Foucault, historical memories are constantly refashioned to suit present purposes. They are also socially acquired and collective. Individual memories gradually fold together into a collective memory of the group. Embedded in the social fabric, they become idealized memories and their ability to survive in the face of alternative memories, or counter memories, depends on the power of the group that holds them.[1]

Every society has its own regime of truth. Foucault's concept of genealogy traces the development of ideas, culture, and society through history.

People are shaped by place, circumstance and happenings. They are shaped to their environment and society around them. However, both environments and society are constantly changing. Therefore, history too changes shape. Foucault in his genealogy clearly explains how subjects emerge in history through practices of power relations. 'And this is what I would call genealogy, that is, a form of history which can account for the constitution of knowledges, discourses, domains of objects etc., without having to make reference to a subject.'[2] Foucault's notion of 'genealogy' is his substitute for history in its traditional guise.

---

[1] Michael J. Hogan. *Hiroshima in History and Memory*. Cambridge University Press, 1996, p. 4. Michel Foucault (1926–1984) was a French philosopher and historian. A social critic, he is among the most influential of twentieth century thinkers.

[2] Philip Barker. *Michel Foucault*. Edinburgh University Press, 1998, p. 22.

So, what is history? History is more than just the story of the past. In one sense, it is a total accumulation and continuous record of events, an unending dialogue between the present and the past. It is the totality of past events. In another, since history is especially related to human affairs, one may say that history reflects the society that writes it. These are shaped by current concerns. According to nineteenth century British historian Edward Hallett Carr, history, '... consciously or unconsciously, reflects our position in time, and forms part of our answer to the broader question what view we take of the society in which we live.'[3] All historical facts come to us as a result of interpretative choices by historians. However, the historian is of his own age, belonging not to the past but to the present, bound by the conditions of current human existence. 'The very words which he uses—words like democracy, empire, war, revolution—have current connotations from which he cannot divorce them.'[4]

In France, according to Foucault, the word *history* means two things: what historians talk about and what historians do in their practice. As Foucault puts it, it is through the practice of historians that history 'transforms documents into monuments.' These monuments, or symbolic markers, a textual body, often statues, structures or buildings, serve as lasting reminders in society to commemorate or celebrate national accomplishments. Some of these material 'reminders' in society will be further discussed in part 3. At school, one is taught about the great things in history that one should know about and remember so as not to forget their history past. In order to 'make history' though, one must do something memorable, or of relevance to the society writing the history.

Japan, which traces its history beyond two thousand years, boasts a cavalcade of men whom the once ruling elites elevated to the status of national heroes. Among these are Oda Nobunaga, Toyotomi Hideyoshi, and Tokugawa Ieyasu. Each of these 'heroes' acquired concrete expression in one or more shrines because of their rendered significance on the national terrain. Reunifying the war torn country while defending the imperial institution against the *bakufu*, rendered sixteenth century warlords Oda Nobunaga and Toyotomi Hideyoshi significant by placing them among the official pantheon of heroes.[5]

---

[3]   Edward Carr. *What is History?* Macmillan, London, 1961, p. 8.

[4]   Ibid., pp. 24–5

[5]   Bakufu - the name given to the Shogun's government.

豊臣秀吉画像
（高台寺蔵）

A popular image of *Kampaku* Hideyoshi (Kodaiji Temple)

Taken by Katrice

Takashi Fujitani, professor of modern history at the University of California, mentions in his research on nationalism how in 1868 Emperor Meiji himself had shrines erected to Oda Nobunaga and Toyotomi Hideyoshi. Oda's shrine was in Kyoto, *Kenkun Jinja*, Toyotomi's shrine in the same city, *Toyokuni Jinja*, and a branch shrine to Hideyoshi in Osaka were all completed in 1880.

Hideyoshi's family crest, Toyotomi (Toyokuni Shrine)

Taken by Katrice

THE LEGITIMATION OF POWER: THE ADOPTION OF COURT CULTURE

The Japanese medieval world was characterized by a dual power structure: the new samurai power and the older emperor's court. This basic structure was formally institutionalized when the samurai established a semi-central regime, commonly called the *bakufu*, or shogunate. Beginning with the Kamakura shogunate in the late twelfth century, medieval Japanese history until the sixteenth century was marked by the gradual expansion of the samurai's power and the corresponding decline of the aristocracy's.[6]

From the late twelfth century until well into the nineteenth century, the samurai, or military class, were the most important and powerful political actors in Japanese society. No other East Asian society experienced such a long-lasting domination by its warrior class. Power over land descended upon those able to muster and control military force. The control of military force depended upon strict and independent administration of the lands a lord could take. Sengoku warriors, the samurai, had thus secured imperial revenues and sustained the dignity of the court, and consequently the emperor, for the sake of their own legitimacy.

While the nobility lost most of its influence, the pageantry of court remained a symbol of political decorum. The shogunate remained the source of military authority. *Daimyo* lords absorbed numerous villages and their proprietors into a new political constellation centered upon themselves. Hideyoshi's first lord, Imagawa Yoshimoto, was a *shugo*, or military governor, and a brilliant administrator. Hideyoshi's second lord, Oda Nobunaga, was a clever and brilliant warrior. As warring states *daimyo*, both the Oda and the Imagawa armies met the same challenge: 'to subordinate villages and their armed cultivators, as well as local military proprietors with rights to those villages, to their own control. The Oda did this through battle, the Imagawa through their courts of law.'[7]

HIDEYOSHI: THE ANTECEDENT OF A HERO

It is important to explore the society and the armies Hideyoshi entered and the consequential experiences and events that influenced and shaped such a humble man of peasant origins, who was denied both wealth and pedigree at birth. Bonds between a lord and his soldiers were the essential expression of authority.

In *Discipline and Punish*, Foucault believed that authority, or power, was not a thing to be held and used by a sole individual or group. Rather, he perceived it as both a complex flow and a set of relations between

---

6   Eiko Ikegami. *The Taming of the Samurai*. Harvard University Press, Cambridge, 1995, p. 48

7   Ibid., p. 27.

different groups and areas of society, which changes with circumstances and time. The other point Foucault makes about power is that it is not solely negative (working to control or repress people), but also that it is highly productive. For example, in the way it produces what we are and what we can do and how we perceive our position in the world.

In spite of his lord's power, yet not in defiance, after several years of loyal service, Hideyoshi left the Imagawa in 1558 to join Oda Nobunaga. Reasons as to why he shifted lords remain uncertain. However, realizing Nobunaga's growing strength, presumably it was a strategic move on Hideyoshi's part, as Nobunaga was known across the realm as the most powerful daimyo in all central Japan. Or, perhaps the authority, or power, enforced on Hideyoshi by Imagawa was a positive force, influential to Hideyoshi in realizing his own ability and skill. Nobunaga was also the warrior whom Hideyoshi had admired and respected for a long time.

Hideyoshi's relationship with Nobunaga lasted just over twenty four years, from their meeting in 1558 until Nobunaga's death in 1582. Based upon stories of the *Mino Campaign*, it is understood that Hideyoshi won early favor and support from Nobunaga for his loyalty and bravery. According to Berry, he surpassed Nobunaga's senior retainers in valor and displayed unusual tactical skill. He also startled everyone with an intelligence that belied his origins.[8]

'It is a very consoling reflection for a soul like mine, little disposed to great actions, to think that fidelity to little things may, by an imperceptible progress, raise us to the most eminent sanctity: because little things lead to greater…'[9]

Even Toyotomi Hideyoshi's exact birth year remains indistinct. Most records of Hideyoshi say he was born in 1536, yet some proclaim he was born in 1537. He died in 1598. Wherever Hideyoshi's true origins lie, one thing remains true and that is the certainty that he rose from the fields of the peasant farmer, to the lowest rank of the samurai hierarchy, gradually elevating himself through self-legitimation to the rank of the highest Japanese warlord. It can be said without a doubt that here, little things *did* lead to greater.

The Muromachi Period (1339–1568) was one of great artistic merit for Japan, though it was marred by a series of bloody domestic wars, culminating in what became known as the *Sengoku Jidai*, 'the time of the country at war', during which there emerged the three great warriors— Nobunaga, Hideyoshi and Ieyasu—who between them brought unity to a divided nation and laid the foundations of an enduring peace. In history, they are known and remembered as the 'Unifiers of Japan'.

---

8   Nobunaga embarked on a series of raids upon Mino (now Southern Gifu Prefecture) between 1559 and 1567. This was known as the *Mino Campaign* as discussed in Berry's book *Hideyoshi*.

9   Alan Sheridan (Trans.) quoting Michel Foucault in *Discipline and Punish. The Birth of the Prison*. 'Part Three Discipline. 1. Docile Bodies.' Vintage Books, 1979, p. 140.

In probably the most turbulent age of Japanese history, as depicted in Japanese junior high school textbooks, comics and samurai film, the *Sengoku Jidai* (1467–1568), –Toyotomi Hideyoshi emerged. Historians call this period 'Sengoku', the era of 'the country at war' because it encompassed rebellion—independent domains meant a breakdown of central control, an open resistance to authority against a traditional concept of rule. The whole country was in a state of anarchy where neither military action nor local defiance of the government was new to this age. Hideyoshi came to maturity during the latter half of this warring period. Hideyoshi joined Nobunaga's army as a young man and rose rapidly to become the ablest general of his time.

The son of a lowly foot soldier from peasant stock, he had risen from obscurity. Becoming an *ashigaru*, or foot soldier like his father before him, he joined the ranks at the bottom of the warrior hierarchy. It was from this category that Toyotomi Hideyoshi emerged as one of the greatest figures of Japanese history, quickly working his way up through the ranks to take the highest position in the realm, *Taiko*—the great ruler.

By the time Hideyoshi left home to seek his fortune in the 1550s, all the commonplaces of an earlier day had been discarded: the emperor and his shogunal surrogates had been denied practical authority over the nation; the state was atomized by the competing warlords who created their own autonomous domains; land was distributed by local powers in exchange for military service; and law was rewritten by individual lords to declare their primacy and the eclipse of higher tribunals.[10]

10 Mary Elizabeth Berry. *Hideyoshi*. Harvard University Press, Cambridge (Massachusetts) and London, 1982, p. 17.

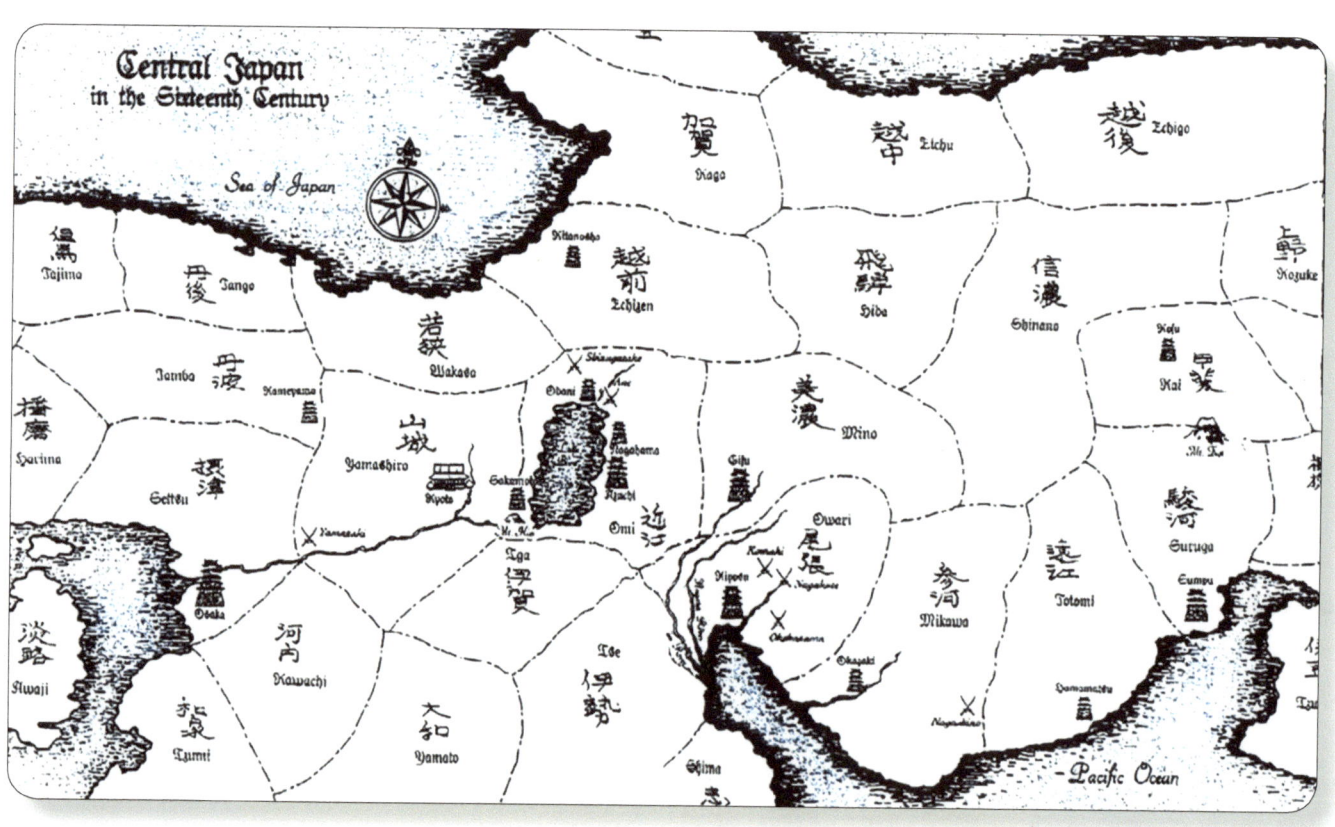

Central Japan in the Sixteenth Century. Notice the size of Osaka Castle compared to the others.

The samurai were a self-confident martial class that compromised approximately ten percent of the population yet dominated Japanese society for seven hundred years. The word at the heart of the warrior's ethical code is 'service'. The very word *samurai* is written with a Chinese character, which means 'one who serves' (侍). Samurai were self- disciplined and devoted. Samurais were elites. A samurai in full armor, resolute in the service of his feudal lord, presented an awesome sight.

> 'For most people, indeed, the very idea of a *corps d'elite* suggests high handed and insensitive arrogance. Historical models abound: Norman barons, Spanish hildalgos, Prussian officers. In their company must be included the *bushi*, or warrior class of Japan, commonly known as samurai.'[11]

Among his measures for pacifying the state, it was under Hideyoshi's dictatorship that samurai power reached its most ostentatious development- creation of the samurai class. Samurai honor embraced the ideal of personal integrity and included, therefore, some notion of free will and even of the importance of the individual. Honor, for what seemed to be a forgotten word, is what samurai willed to risk their lives for their feudal lord.

While competence in the military arts and plain courage were taken for granted as two fundamental constituents in the character of every samurai, it would be a crude mistake, of course, to imagine that the samurai regime did nothing else but fight or prepare for battle. It was, after all, for seven centuries the ruling class of Japan and was therefore heavily engaged in national and local administration at every level above that of the rural village. This administration was very much government for, as well as by, the warrior class. This did not necessarily mean that the common man found government invariably oppressive, but even at the best of times he had to tread warily.

'In feudal societies, power functioned essentially through signs and levies. Signs of loyalty to the feudal lords, rituals, ceremonies, and so forth, and levies in the form of taxes, pillage, hunting, war, etc.'[12] Hideyoshi's power functioned evidently through signs. For instance, invitations to attend his tea ceremonies, a show of status by presenting others with gifts, and through his abundant décor of lavish Momoyama art that decorated his castle. Levies existed in the forms of various taxes, as they do today, yet Hideyoshi also used state infrastructure accompanied with the labor of his retainers to build his magnificent Osaka Castle.

---

[11]   Richard Storry. *The Way of the Samurai*. Orbis Publishing Limited, London, 1978, p. 7.

[12]   Paul Rabinow. *The Foucault Reader*. Pantheon Books, New York, 1984, p. 66. Quoting Michel Foucault in Colin Gordon, *Power/Knowledge: Selected Interviews and Other Writings, 1972–1977*, Harvester Press, Ltd, 1980.

WHAT IT MEANT TO BE SAMURAI

Hideyoshi under his *Daimyo*, or feudal lord, Oda Nobunaga, would learn well what it meant to be a samurai. Of course, the samurai protected their homes and families, but their true glory came on the battlefield, defending their lord against enemies. Born the son of a daimyo in 1534, Nobunaga's reign, though short, had an immense impact on Japan. Lord of Nagoya Castle, he destroyed opposing clans in brilliant campaigns against superior forces. He was the first *daimyo* general to adopt the newly imported Western muskets. He gradually gained control of the region around the capital of Kyoto, which he took in 1568. In 1580, he became master of all central Japan.

Nobunaga continued to amass power, but before he could subdue the whole country, he was betrayed and caught off guard one night by a rebellious vassal,[13] Akechi Mitsuhide. The life of the most powerful warlord in Japan ended by ritual suicide, "seppuku"[14] in 1582. Ruthless and feared upon the mere mention of his name, Nobunaga was the first to begin the unification of war torn Japan. A unification which Hideyoshi would later complete in 1590, continuing Nobunaga's work of conquest thirty years after it began. It is important to understand Nobunaga 'the warrior' first in order to better understand Hideyoshi because Nobunaga was so influential in the 'making' of Hideyoshi 'the warrior'. At the same time it is also important to understand how society was shaped during the rule of the military rulers before Hideyoshi entered the realm.

In an age of treachery, turmoil and civil wars, warriors ruled by birthright and sword. The sword was the symbol of the samurai class, as, only they were allowed to carry a sword. This was a rule introduced by Hideyoshi, a necessary order that enabled him to create *his* samurai system. All samurai carried two swords, a short sword and a long sword, by which they ruled over the farmers and the peasants. The samurai sword was used to enact justice. Power was achieved by the sword, but then had to be legitimated by appropriating the signs of rightful rule. Japan's was an unusual pattern of social and cultural development within East Asia. China and Korea, for instance, usually placed higher prestige on literature and the arts than the military. By contrast, even after the samurai became the rulers of the country, they often found it difficult to convert themselves into either court aristocrats or totally civilized social elites like the Confucian upper classes in other East Asian states.

Violence for the samurai, often by the sword or bow, became the tool through which they could not only extend their sphere of domination but also legitimate their social existence. Japanese democratic society respected the samurai as those who had the power to resolve conflicts and 'keep the peace'. They were therefore

---

[13]   A vassal was someone in feudal times who received protection and land from a lord in return for homage and allegiance.

[14]   "Seppuku" is a ritual form of committing suicide by disembowelment and could only be conducted by a samurai. Behind this gruesome act lies the concept in Japanese thinking that an honorable death is more desirable than living a life in shame.

entitled to govern the country because of their superior military power and peace-keeping ability. They ruled because of their power, yet they had to also prove their entitlement to do so. This is why legitimation was needed. Becoming a samurai and learning the way of the warrior was dependent on lineal descent. Warriors who were not of direct line ancestry were allowed to be subservient samurai yet were tabooed by the imperial court at ever becoming a *shogun*, the great general who ruled over government in feudal Japan. In this age, pedigree was an important factor—it lent an air of legitimacy to naked power.

THE ATTAINMENT OF POWER AND 'SOCIAL CLIMBING'

Timing and strategy guided the samurai. For instance, when Tokugawa Ieyasu's master, Matsudaira, was killed, Ieyasu strategically aligned himself with his master's murderer, Oda Nobunaga. Similarly, Nobunaga's loyal general Toyotomi Hideyoshi seized the moment by murdering the murderer of his own lord, in 1582, immediately giving him the right in essence to claim Nobunaga's vast coalition of army. It was Hideyoshi's nature to act quickly and decisively in order to assert his authority, thereby gaining further support and respect. Ieyasu opposed this ideal. Rather, he was a patient strategist who waited for things to go his way before he would act. Upon Nobunaga's death, Ieyasu chose to subordinate himself to Hideyoshi instead of fighting for control. He obviously realized there was more to be gained as Hideyoshi's ally than as his enemy.

The presence Hideyoshi now had on Japanese society is reflected in Foucault's concept of the nexus between power and knowledge. Foucault's thought explored the shifting patterns of power within a society and the ways in which power relates to the self. Hideyoshi, who was nothing if not ingenious as a genealogist (using the term in a non- Focauldian way), also assumed his master's courtly name of *Taira* when he succeeded to Nobunaga's hegemony. In order to legitimate his power, Hideyoshi reached for still greater heights and worked energetically to institutionalize his military power into a national government. Grafting his power onto the social prestige of the high nobility, he succeeded to national hegemony by legitimating himself through the title of *kampaku*, Imperial Regent, and by his close proximity to the throne.

No member of the military had ever before assumed the title of *kampaku*, or Imperial Regent. In order to obtain it, Hideyoshi had to prove himself of *Fujiwara* descent, which he did ingeniously. *Fujiwara* was one of the four classical noble houses—*Fujiwara*, *Tachibana*, *Taira*, and *Minamoto*—each with long enduring histories of 920, 850, 800, and 750 years respectively. Hideyoshi arranged to have himself adopted as the son of a former *kampaku*, 'thereby breaking and entering the Fujiwara monopoly on the office, his absorption into the courtly mode became complete'.[15] This 'borrowed lineage', however, reminded Hideyoshi of his own lack of family background.

---

15   George Elison. 'Hideyoshi, The Bountiful Minister,' in G. Elison and B. L. Smith, eds, *Warlords, Artists and Commoners*. University Press of Hawaii, 1981, p. 232.

Like Nobunaga, Hideyoshi never took the title of *shogun*. He preferred the imperial distinction of a title in the old court hierarchy. After all, the emperor was the only one who could recognize 'power' and appoint a *shogun*. Without 'paramount pedigree' or 'true' lineage, there was no way this 'position' could be granted.

Despite this, Hideyoshi was granted the name Toyotomi (豊臣) by imperial decree in 1585. This name historically remains and literally translates as 'bountiful minister'.

ARMS AND ARTS

Toyotomi Hideyoshi set an example in the construction and decoration of his castles, as his predecessor Nobunaga had done, that was decidedly ostentatious and considered impressive by European standards. According to Japanese historian George Elison, this display of wealth 'cultured' the samurai. Yet, it was not considered fitting that a samurai should give himself wholly to the pursuit of scholarly or artistic excellence if this meant that his skill as a fighting man might be impaired. Maintaining a balance by continuous practice of the military arts and the code of morality and conduct perculiar to the samurai, Hideyoshi progressed in civility and social decorum. The samurai, over the centuries of their rule, established a code of conduct, which came to be known around 1900 as *Bushido*, the way of the warrior. This code was drawn from Confucianism, Shinto and Buddhism.

Confucianism required the samurai to show absolute loyalty to his lord. Towards the oppressed he was expected to show benevolence and exercise justice. From Buddhism, the samurai learnt the lesson that life is impermanent, a handy reason to face death with serenity. Shinto provided the samurai with patriotic beliefs in the divine status both of the emperor and of Japan, the abode of the gods. These were the 'rules of conduct' by which a warrior lived. As a result of these 'rules' the warrior, sometimes despite himself, tended to acquire the cultural attribute of the court noble.

Tea ceremony and Noh drama were popular practices amongst the nobility at the time of Hideyoshi's 'rise'. The tea ceremony brought the samurai into a quietist dimension wholly removed from the exigencies of combat or of training and practice in the martial arts. Inspired and developed by Zen monks, the ritual of the tea ceremony provided the samurai with a refreshment of the spirit that settled the mind before battle and induced tranquility at any time.

For Hideyoshi, it proved him a 'cultured' man to the emperor when he hosted a glamorous five day tea ceremony in his honor at his recently constructed Juraku Palace in 1588. This imperial visit was indeed the crowning event of Hideyoshi's aristocratization.

As Elison puts it, what status required, Hideyoshi acquired. When he became *kampaku*, he took instruction in *waka*, poetry, just as naturally as he took instruction from his lords or court nobles. He was a 'cultured samurai', often acting the lead role on stage publicly of what had become 'dignified theatre'—Noh drama. In all he could, and *did* do, Hideyoshi strived for cultural accomplishment. He evidently personified the combination of 'arms' and 'arts'.

HIDEYOSHI'S REGIME OF TRUTH

The transition from a commoner with no family name to the magnificence of the 'Bountiful Minister Toyotomi' is nothing short of 'heroic'. Self-legitimized, he created a new life and a new world within the prevailing *Regime of Truth*. This regime was a structure, which ruled society, government and business.

> Each society has its regime of truth, its 'general politics' of truth: that is, the types of discourse which it accepts and makes function as true; the mechanisms and instances which enable one to distinguish true and false statements, the means by which each is sanctioned; the techniques and procedures accorded value in the acquisition of truth; the status of those who are charged with saying what counts as true.[16]

As Foucault explains, 'regime of truth' supplies the mechanisms used for deciding what is true and the status of those who offer 'true' statements and the criteria by which truth and legitimation are determined. In *Discipline and Punish*, Foucault's notion of truth is strongly related to power. As Foucault explains it, truth is linked in a circular relation with systems of power, which produce and sustain it, and to effects of power, which it induces and which extend it. *A Regime of Truth*. Hideyoshi's power was a result of his fabricated 'truths', however, without such, 'our hero', the brilliant general as we know him, would not have created a 'space' for himself amidst the tales of feudal Japan.

Oda Nobunaga accepted Toyotomi Hideyoshi by making him one of his top generals. Hideyoshi's power became so great that even the emperor had no choice but to accept him, bestowing upon him the title of *Kampaku*, his Imperial Regent. In fact, regardless of status, all of sixteenth century Japanese society accepted Toyotomi Hideyoshi as the tactical, loyal and clever warlord who had at last unified the warring states for them, consequently pacifying the realm. Born into a peasant farming family, perhaps Hideyoshi was just the person 'needed' to complete the unification of a nation who 'lives off the land'?

Today, it is his legacy that remains 'needed' to inspire and encourage individuals living in a now modern Japanese democratic society, into believing and pursuing the fundamentals of the basic Japanese work ethic— that based on the ideals of discipline and hard work, anybody can attain greatness if they strive hard enough to achieve it!

---

16   Paul Rabinow. The Foucault Reader. Pantheon Books, New York, 1984, p. 73.

(二)

HIDEYOSHI AND OSAKA CASTLE: STRENGTH, ARTISTRY AND CULTURE

Looking at a map of Japan, one can notice how part of the archipelago is split in half from west to east by the Seto Inland Sea. Osaka lies at the eastern end of this natural waterway and was the political and economic center of Japan from ancient times. The city has changed over the centuries but has always remained a vital center of commerce in Japan. Canal transport has fostered the establishment of a number of profitable businesses. Many companies started in Osaka, and then developed markets around the world.

Oda Nobunaga gained control of the entire Osaka area near the end of the sixteenth century as a consequence of a decade of fighting in his campaign to unify Japan. After his demise, Toyotomi Hideyoshi inherited his unifying mission, built Osaka Castle and promoted commerce in the region, thereby increasing the wealth of this already prosperous area.

In the late twentieth century, Osaka experienced another revival. Centuries ago, it flourished because of its location by the sea. These days the coast is again full of activity—the Bay Area Development Project extends Osaka's influence westward into the sea, with Kansai International Airport now operating on reclaimed land in the bay. Due to its prime location, Osaka has the potential to become Japan's gateway to Asia once more.

One of the most visited places in Osaka is Osaka Castle, coming only second to Universal Studios. The grandness of the castle attracts many visitors, which can undoubtedly be attributed to the restorative work done on the castle that was completed in 1997. At that time, it was restored to the beautiful appearance of the original castle, which was built by Toyotomi Hideyoshi.

Today the castle stands as a glittering symbol of Osaka surrounded by other important buildings, such as the Osaka International Peace Center and Osaka Castle Hall. Altogether, these structures have contributed to the development of a truly grand international park featuring important historical remains.

As the power center of his regime, Hideyoshi built his castle on the site of the former Ishiyama Honganji that Nobunaga had captured from the True Pure Land Sect in 1580 after just over a decade of intense fighting. Today, Osaka Castle is literally full of Hideyoshi history and culture, seemingly a never-ending one at that. However, the external appearance and shape and even the *rule* of this castle has changed quite significantly with the times, up to the present day. It was completed in approximately 1590 as a display of grandeur after accomplishing his goal of unifying Japan.

Castle as a Sign of Authority: Nobunaga at Azuchi

Ishiyama Honganji (the head monastic center for the *Ikko* sect of Buddhism) existed on the site before Osaka Castle. Built in 1496, this was the primary fortress of the *Ikko-ikki*, armies of warrior monks and peasants who opposed samurai rule. It acted as a cathedral-fortress and was considered impenetrable, due largely to its location and orientation. Defending their location against a brutal takeover, at any one time more than one hundred monks were on patrol, and upwards of ten thousand could be summoned to battle simply by ringing a bell.

The area's topography—rivers, mountains and sea coast—had obviously been the deciding factor in choosing this location. Their advantages and disadvantages had been considered, and the comparative difficulties of attack and defenses together with other logistical problems had all been thought out. With the prosperous mercantile city of Sakai close by, Osaka was conveniently connected with numerous trade routes to China, Korea and Southeast Asia. Meanwhile, the nearby Yamato and Kawachi mountain chains formed a natural defensive wall.

Sakai lies at the eastern end of the Seto Inland Sea, comfortably within today's Osaka Municipal Prefecture. It was initially famous for its ironwork, and by the sixteenth century, most of Japan's guns were manufactured there, thus making Sakai an important center for production. Besides guns, swords were also manufactured in this castle town.

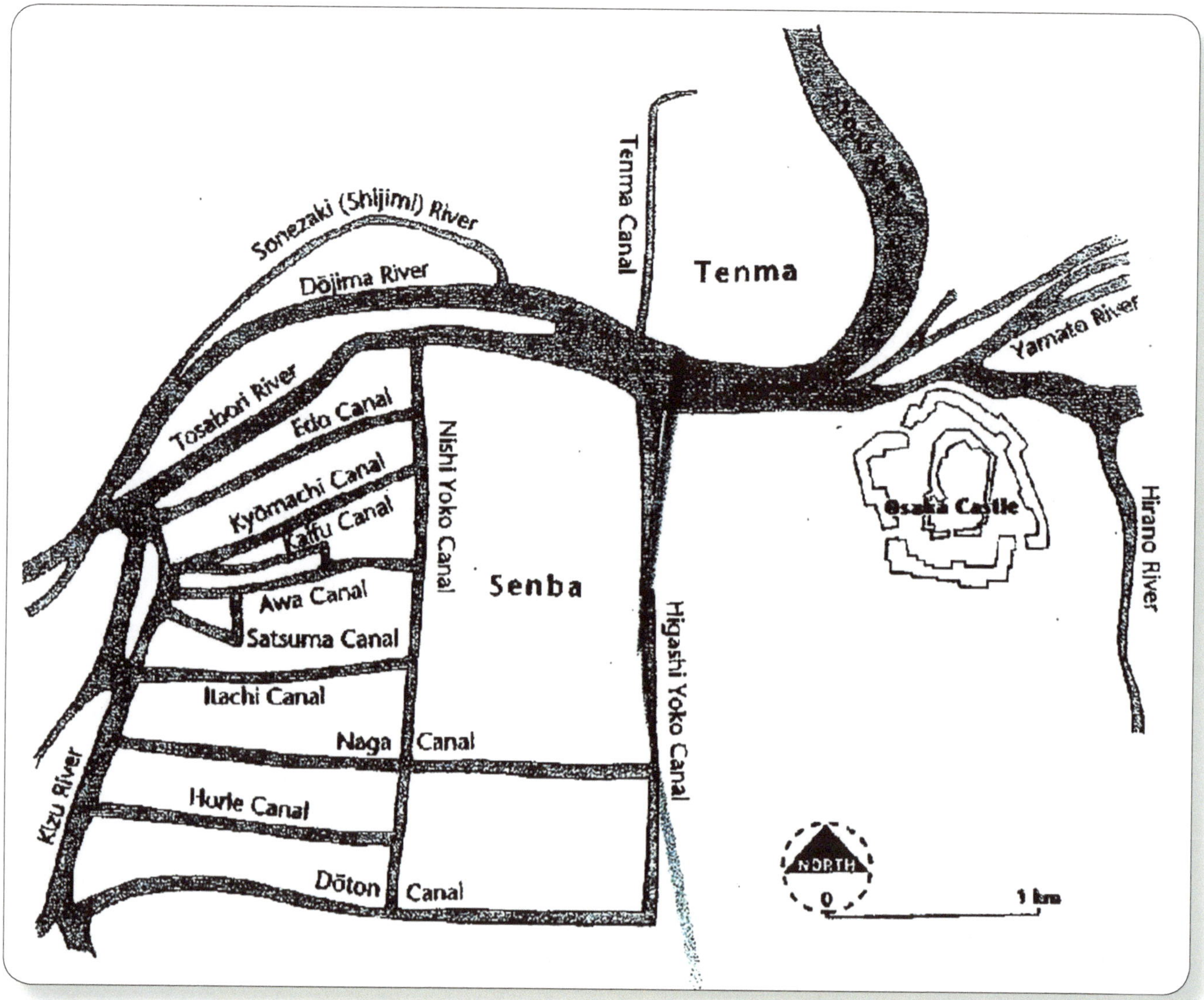

Major waterways within Osaka (late sixteenth century).

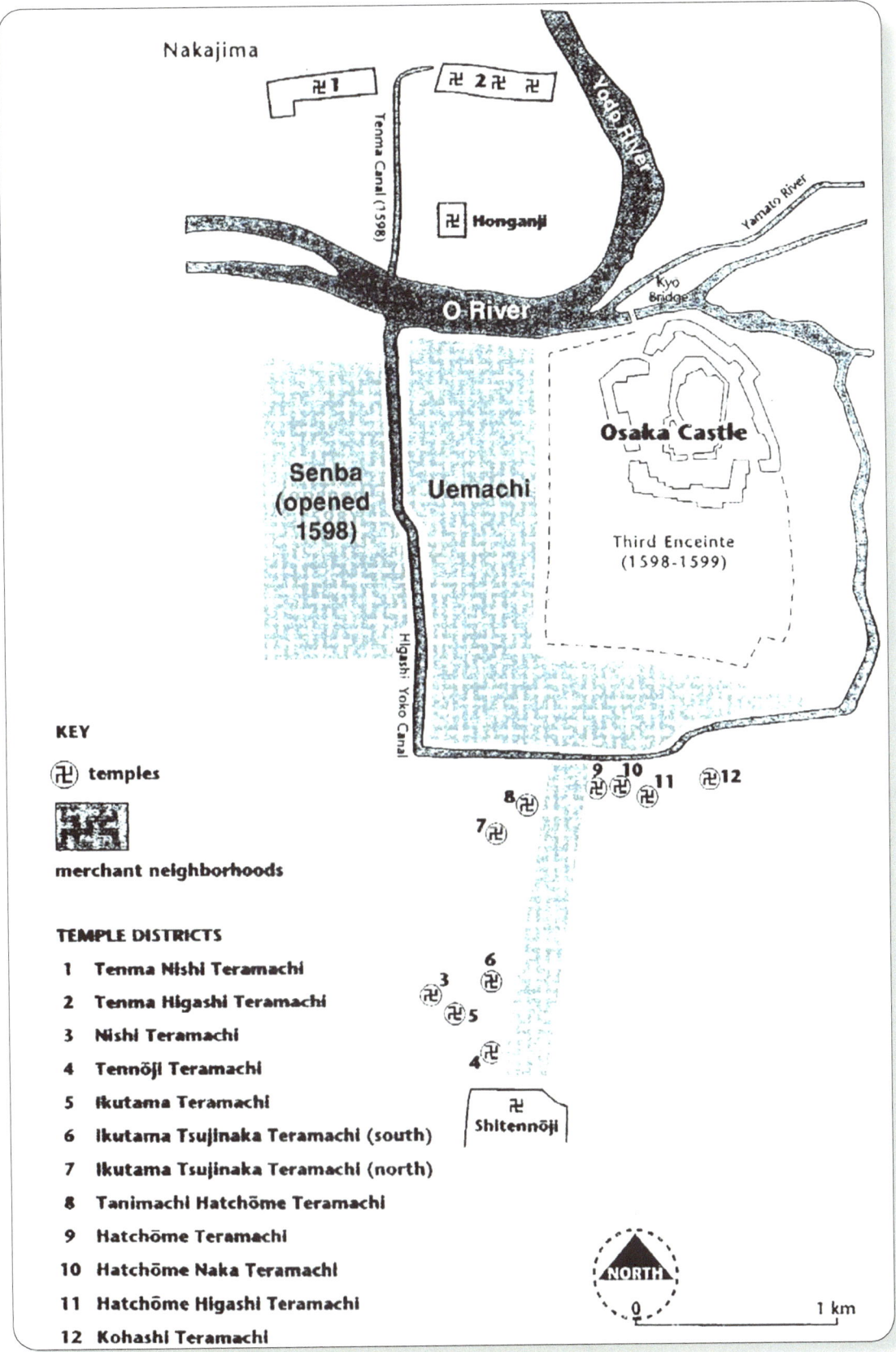

Osaka under Toyotomi Hideyoshi.

KEY

卍 temples

merchant neighborhoods

TEMPLE DISTRICTS

1 Tenma Nishi Teramachi
2 Tenma Higashi Teramachi
3 Nishi Teramachi
4 Tennōji Teramachi
5 Ikutama Teramachi
6 Ikutama Tsujinaka Teramachi (south)
7 Ikutama Tsujinaka Teramachi (north)
8 Tanimachi Hatchōme Teramachi
9 Hatchōme Teramachi
10 Hatchōme Naka Teramachi
11 Hatchōme Higashi Teramachi
12 Kohashi Teramachi

'Sakai's handicraft industries included printing, brewing, and the production of damask and bleached cotton.'[17]

Sakai City was of great strategic importance and a factor as to why Osaka's position, relative to the city, was sought after. Not only was it a prosperous mercantile city, but also the city where Nobunaga decided to start the trade policy with Europe, as guns were purchased from the Portugese in Sakai.

> Sakai was not only an important merchant city, but it was also a natural port closed to the Imperial and Shogunal bases. Therefore, the city's important geographical location as well as its volume of goods traded there, allowed Sakai's oligarchy of wealthy and politically connected merchants (*Gosho*) to self govern the city by determining its economic policies and by perpetuating its wealth. Basically everything was traded in Sakai. There were pawnbrokers, money exchange and money laundering places.[18]

In his policy of unification, Nobunaga was occupied in warfare by eliminating major obstacles, such as the big institution of Ishiyama and other temples which resisted unification.

The Ishiyama Honganji came under siege from the forces of Nobunaga between 1570 and 1580, but it managed to hold out for eleven years, making it the longest battle in Japanese history. The battle ceased in 1580 only when the emperor intervened.

Unable to take over this prime location, Nobunaga settled for another location. It is noted in Eiji Yoshikawa's *Taiko* that Lord Nobunaga had his eye on Osaka for a number of years. However, since the warrior monks of the Honganji were entrenched in their temple-fortress there, he was forced to settle for Azuchi.

> The majesty of the Japanese castle, its formidable strength, the grandeur of its spectacle, the infinite subtlety of its crafted decoration, created monuments as ageless as ambition itself.[19]

Also strategically located across the main trade routes to the north and east, Azuchi Castle was built on the east shore of Lake Biwa east of Kyoto in 1579 before Osaka Castle was even planned. Azuchi Castle was incomparable in strength. It was therefore Nobunaga's lead that Hideyoshi followed, which announced the beginning of an entirely new epoch in castle construction.

---

[17]   James McClain. *Osaka. The Merchants' Capital of Early Modern Japan.* Cornell University, USA, 1999, p. 39.

[18]   Maria Petrucci. 'Tea Politics, Christianity, Diplomacy and the Economics of the Korean Wars: Shimai Soshitsu and Kamiya Sotan's Roles in the Process of Japan's State Formation Between 1570 and 1600.' pp. 11–12.

[19]   William Coaldrake. 'The Symbol and Substance of Momoyama and Early Edo Authority,' in *Architecture and Authority in Japan.* Routledge, London, 1996, p. 137.

HIDEYOSHI'S OSAKA CASTLE

The construction of Hideyoshi's Osaka Castle began in 1583, one year after Nobunaga's death, and lasted approximately seven years. It is often said in Western history books that Hideyoshi modelled his castle on Nobunaga's Azuchi Castle yet surpassed it in every way, especially in its location. Osaka Castle was, as mentioned, very strategically located. 'As the location of the country's most important castle and a place from which to rule the nation, Osaka was many times superior to Nobunaga's Azuchi.'[20]

Four hundred and forty years have passed since Toyotomi Hideyoshi began building Osaka Castle and the surrounding castle town in 1583. Around this castle developed the port city of Osaka, which began expanding as a trading center at the end of the sixteenth century. Modern day Osaka originated directly from this site. During his reign from Osaka Castle, Hideyoshi set up a central administrative network in Osaka, brought the century-long civil wars to a close, and established the powerful Toyotomi Government, which through his well-calculated legislation, reshaped Japanese society as we know it today.

Under Hideyoshi, Osaka represented a prototype for what became an entire category of urban settlement, the castle town. Following Hideyoshi's lead, between the 1580s and the 1620s, more than two hundred castle towns later emerged across Japan. According to Japanese history professor at Brown University James McClain, the vitality of the urban experience in the medieval period provided an important legacy for early modern Japan that still survives today. The importance of commercial wealth and symbiotic centrality of the warrior-merchant relationship appears to have been well understood by Hideyoshi, recognizing that his regime could share the benefits to be gained from trade and production. Through trade, merchants gained profits and a great deal of reputation, while the warrior (*bushi*) gained prestige. Consequently, Hideyoshi encouraged merchants from around the country to set up their businesses in the city, which soon prospered.

During this time of economic growth, some of Japan's business dynasties were founded. One whose name still reigns strong is *Mitsui- Sumitomo Bank*. Some of the more familiar modern companies based in Osaka are *Asahi Shimbun* (media), *Matsushita Electric Industrial Co., Ltd.* (electric appliances, data devices), *Mizuno Corporation* (sporting goods) and *Suntory Ltd.* (alcohol).

Social and political life in the latter part of the sixteenth century revolved around three cities: the emperor's city of Kyoto, Tokugawa's city of Edo (now Tokyo), and the commercial center of Osaka. At this time, Edo was a remote castle town. I refer to this as 'Tokugawa's city' because that's where the area of land was that Hideyoshi gave to Tokugawa, a strategic ploy of Hideyoshi's to keep his 'powerful ally' far away from his city of Osaka. In fact, most history books about feudal Japan, or medieval Japan (1185-1600), refer to Osaka as the 'merchant's capital'. It has also been referred to as a regional center of government with vibrant economic life.

---

20   Eiji Yoshikawa. *Taiko*. Kodansha International Limited, Tokyo, 1992, p. 843.

Feudalism brought many changes in Japan. It was a time when powerful warlords and their samurai ruled Japan. The emperor appeared at ceremonies, but had no real control over the people or government. He merely served as a figurehead for the warlords, or shogun, as they ruled in the name of the emperor.

Japanese feudal class structure placed merchants at the bottom of their class system. Confucian ideals emphasized the importance of productivity, so farmers and fisherman had a higher status than merchants, otherwise known as traders and shopkeepers. Although they made up only about ten percent of the population, feudal society was dominated by the samurai warrior class. This was followed by farmers and peasants, artisans (who produced necessary goods like utensils and swords) and lastly merchants.

The merchant class of Japan was not respected for a long time as people thought they were dishonest rogues, looking to cheat them of their hard earned money. However, Merchants were given free hand to set prices for their goods, giving them great autonomy. Since they were self-governed, they often inflated their prices, resulting in immeasurable wealth.

Once the tea ceremony gained a new-found popularity amongst the elites in the 1500s, many merchants "adopted" the tea business as well, turning themselves into tea masters while gaining a new respect from the society. Consequently, it became inevitable that the samurai would now regularly socialize with the rich and dutiful merchants. If today Tokyo is Japan's capital, Osaka might be called its secondary capital. Osaka was where the merchants made and lost their fortunes. To this day, Osakans still greet each other with *moukarimakka?* (Are you making money?) Or, *katteimasuka?* (Are you winning?)

Osaka's merchant heritage positioned it well for industrial growth. Iron, steel, fabrics, ships, heavy and light machinery and chemicals all became part of its output. As a result, the region today accounts for 25 percent of Japan's industrial product and 40 percent of the nation's exports. According to the official Osaka government tourist information website, since the building of its harbor facilities, Osaka has become a major port in its own right. Relying less on the facilities in Kobe, the city's ferry terminal is the largest in Japan, handling over 60 million passengers a year!

Castles, however, served for an era of unprecedented urban growth in the late sixteenth and early seventeenth centuries. Clearly defining the classes into social estates between wealth, prestige, power and status, Hideyoshi encouraged warriors, clerics, merchants and artisans to move into the area around his citadel, thereby encouraging the 'flowering' of commerce and crafts strategically to his own advantage. He provided each group with a separate residential district so to create a society of discrete social estates defined clearly between wealth, prestige, power and status. Such diverse communities enhanced Hideyoshi's authority by symbolizing his ability to project his power and magnificence, control the economy, organize religion to his will, and dictate the direction of social change.

TOKUGAWA'S DESTRUCTION AND RECONSTRUCTION

The period of Hideyoshi's reign however, was a period of great transition. It was a turbulent and yet exciting era, and the fervor of this time still remains close to the hearts of the people of Japan. His administration lasted a mere fifteen years and ended with his death in 1598. A further seventeen years after his death, Osaka Castle and the castle town were completely destroyed by fire in the Summer War of Osaka in 1615, led by Tokugawa Ieyasu.

Battling for control, the Tokugawa army attacked the castle. An army of 155,000 on the Tokugawa side and 55,000 from the Toyotomi's. The result saw the crushing defeat of the Toyotomi line. During the war, Osaka Castle was burnt down.

The war lasted only about four days. On the last day of the war, knowing they were defeated, Hideyoshi's son and his mother committed suicide. As a result, the Tokugawa clan became the most powerful in Japan and the Toyotomi line ended. Despite this, the Tokugawa clan maintained Osaka as its base.

The Tokugawa Government attempted to completely purge the influence of the Toyotomi family, which was represented by Osaka Castle, to secure its ruling in the west of Japan. The Shogunate, the ruling government, thus had to build a new castle that was more majestic in appearance and larger in scale than Hideyoshi's. The Tokugawa Government ordered feudal lords to participate in the reconstruction. Today, a large number of elaborately carved markings, including family crests, remain on the stone walls of the castle and serve to indicate the individual contributions of feudal lords. It was completed in 1629 with an increased height of about fifteen meters on Hideyoshi's, merely to show that *he* was bigger and more powerful than Hideyoshi. The ground level was also raised and the outer moat was filled in so as to change the castle's original design and grounds as much as possible.

One of the only remaining images of Toyotomi Hideyoshi's original Osaka Castle (Osaka Castle Museum).

Tokugawa's reconstruction (Edo Period).
Notice the increased height on the moat walls.

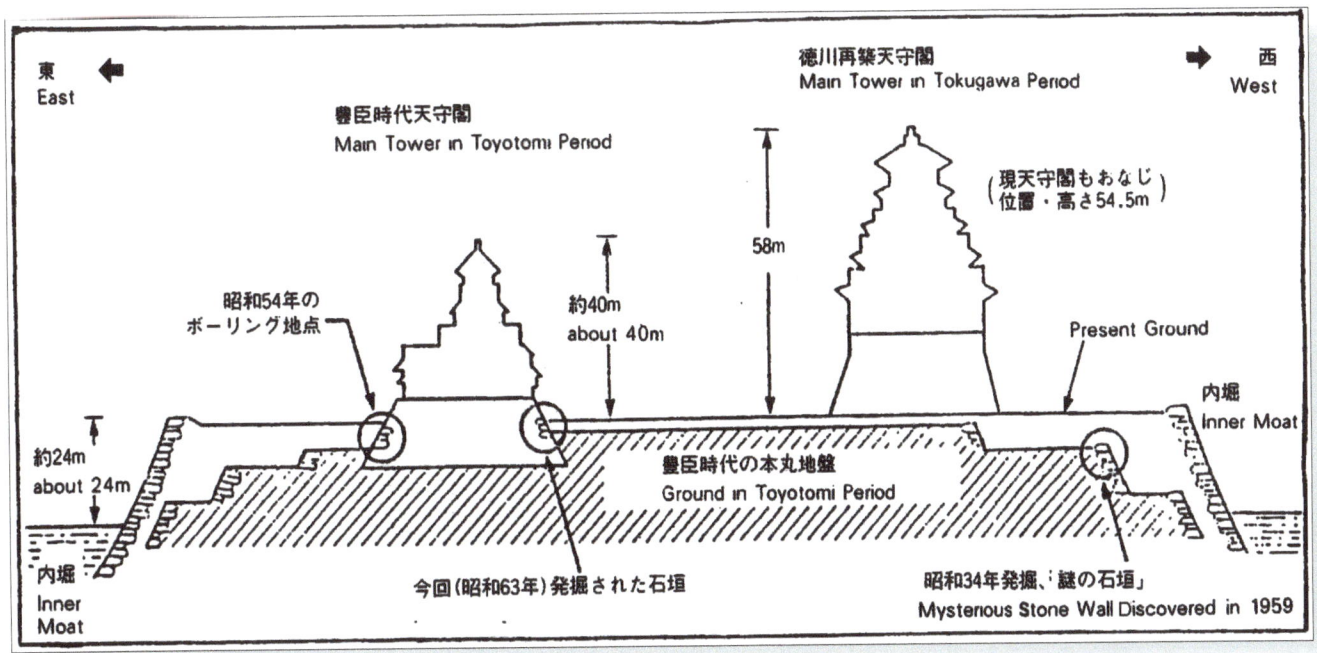

A comparison of the two main towers in two different periods.

Subject to attacks of lightning strikes and even further New Government disturbances due to the transition to the Imperial Restoration during Meiji (1868), Osaka Castle survived the Edo Period (1629–1868), subsequently withstanding the era of feudal rule.

A SYMBOL OF ENDURANCE:
(FROM EDO TO SHOWA 1931)

With the opening of Japan to Western commerce in 1853 and the end of the Tokugawa Shogunate in 1868, Osaka stepped into the forefront of Japan's commerce. At first, Yokohama was the major port for Japan's foreign trade, but after the Great Kanto (Tokyo) Earthquake levelled it in 1923, foreigners looked to Kobe and Osaka as alternative gateways for their import and export businesses.

In 1868 the Tokugawa shogun lost his ruling power and the emperor was restored to the supreme position as the sovereign leader of Japan. This was known as the Meiji Restoration (1868) with Emperor Meiji's ascension to the throne. The Meiji Restoration saw the end of feudal rule, resulting in major political, economic and social change. Although the government still depended upon agriculture for its economy, industrialization was its primary goal. Industrialization was seen as essential for national strength. By adopting it, and installing a national army, the Japanese military could now achieve equality with the Western powers.

Sixty years since the beginning of Meiji saw the main tower of Osaka Castle restored in the Showa Period in 1931. This also was the third time that the main tower was rebuilt. This was the first example in Japan of restoring a building with the technology of the modern age, symbolizing military strength and modern industrial strength. Fittingly, the castle then became home to the regional headquarters for Japan's Imperial Army. It took just over two years to reconstruct Osaka Castle with funds and support coming from the citizens of Osaka.

The reconstruction of the main tower set the goal of reproducing the appearance of the main tower Hideyoshi originally built, making it a permanent monument as well. The work was undertaken by making the most of the building technology available at the time, steel frames and reinforced concrete construction. The height was a staggering 55 meters from the ground, surpassing the original castle by approximately ten meters. At the same time, it was an original idea that the interior of the tower was used to house a local history museum, the only such museum in Osaka. This museum is dedicated to the life of Toyotomi Hideyoshi, Japan's ambitious second unifier, who had now permanently etched his name on the battlefields of history.

1931 reconstruction. Notice the steel frames and huge height, a display of military and industrial strength.

Panoramic photo of Osaka Castle taken during a special large–scale army manoeuvre in November 1932.

The Main Tower stands grandly in the center just one year after its restoration.

Intensive studies of Osaka Castle began ten years after the end of World War II and have continued up to the present day. According to Osaka Tourist Association, relics and other remains buried underground have systematically been excavated, and historical records and charts have also been discovered. Historical materials, in particular those related to Hideyoshi and Osaka Castle, have been continuously collected since the castle was rebuilt from donations by Osaka citizens in 1931. Thus the history of Hideyoshi's Osaka Castle has gradually been brought back to life.

In 1980–81, Osaka Tourist Association held an exhibition entitled 'Hideyoshi and Osaka Castle' in a number of cities throughout Japan. Since the exhibition, Osaka Castle Tourist Information has said that many new articles have been uncovered in and around the castle. Naturally, studies on these findings have also been undertaken. Furthermore, in order to meet the requests of foreign visitors to Osaka Castle Museum, since 1988 the exhibits have been explained both in Japanese and English.

Since the 1950s, the castle grounds and its thirteen buildings and structures, including several turrets, a tea house and gates, have been designated as valuable cultural assets of Japan. The majesty of Osaka Castle, arguably Osaka's biggest and most prominent landmark, whose origin belies bloody power struggles leading up to the 1603 foundation of the Edo era, remains as an Important Cultural Property as well as a designated National Treasure.

HEISEI AND SOCIAL CHANGE

The Heisei Period in Japan (1989-2019), corresponds to the reign of Emperor Akihito. It began when he ascended to the throne on the death of his father and former emperor, Hirohito, who reigned over the preceding Showa Period (1926-1989).

During the years of the Heisei Period 1995–1997, Osaka Castle underwent its most special of all renovations. This renovation was carried out to make the symbol of Osaka even more beautiful and solid before Japan handed it over to the twenty first century. Information provided by the castle museum greatly details the renovation process. Simply put, the exterior was preserved with lots of water-proofing work, removal and cleaning of the copper roof tiles, a corrosion protective covering applied to the concrete, an alkali solution permeated into the interior of concrete to prevent the corrosion of iron frames, and repairing and adding of new layers of gold leaf to the ornamental fixtures.

On the interior, each of the eight floors was renewed. With equal access for all people taken into account, the flow of the visitors was redesigned, lighting of showcases improved, as well as facilities and functions too. On supposition of a level 2 earthquake (severe shock), new walls of earthquake-proof steel plates were installed from the first to fourth floors, which became the principal posts of the tower, and carbon fibre and reinforced rods were coiled onto the pillars and beams for strengthening. I believe such strengthening of the castle is a direct result of the devastating earthquake that destroyed much of nearby Kobe in January 1995. This was during the early stages of the reconstruction project. Again, only this time better, the best in advanced building technology was used. Also, the addition of an elevator meant for the first time that disabled visitors could freely access the inside of the castle.

The year 1981 was the International Year for Disabled Persons. However, Japan's development in this field was slow. According to Shizuoka University of Art and Culture Professor Satoshi Kose, who has researched Japan's position on this topic extensively, it was only in 1993 when the Fundamental Law on Disabled Persons was revised that awareness spread. It was soon after this that Japan had a period with special provisions for wheelchairs, such as elevators for wheelchair-use only and convertible escalators for wheelchairs. Despite this, it was not until the year 2000 that the Accessible Transportation Law came into effect in Japan, making the castle an early manifestation of compliance with the 1993 law.

Today, Osaka Castle is the main tourist attraction for both Japanese nationals and foreigners within the city of Osaka. It is also the largest remaining 'full structure' castle in Japan. As described in information provided by Osaka Castle Museum, Osaka Castle proper and its outer enclosure is about 730,000 square meters and it is an authorized special historical site. However, if the whole of Osaka Castle Park including its environs is considered, the area amounts to about 1,070,000 square meters. There are now thirteen buildings in the precincts constructed in the Edo Period (1603–1867). These buildings together with the 'main keep' (*Tenshukaku*), the museum, and Osaka Castle Hall serve the public's need, either for cultural or sports purposes. Osaka Castle Hall was established in 1983 and still remains the largest hall for sports and music in Western Japan today.

Before and after Heisei renovations.

The newly built elevator (Heisei social change).
Taken by Katrice

Modern aerial views of Osaka Castle and the surrounding city.
Notice the greatness of the castle grounds.

Imperial Regent (*Kampaku*) Hideyoshi.
A gold commemorative telephone card,
celebrating the 400th anniversary (1998) since the death of this great man.
Taken by Katrice

TRANSFER INTO THE CULTURAL

Hideyoshi's dominance in the political and military spheres, as a result of the successful legitimation of himself, transferred also into the cultural. Again, like Nobunaga, he refined himself culturally in the appreciation and practice of the arts. Intellectual and artistic achievement legitimated his position amongst the court nobility and in particular the emperor, in order to gain authority on a much greater level. Assimilation into and 'above' the imperial court and its culture was Hideyoshi's aim. This is evident by the fact that Hideyoshi took the title of *Kampaku*, thereby becoming regent for the adult emperor. Hence, he took it upon himself to 'learn' and 'improve' to a level, which even exceeded his former lord. But, before this, he again followed Nobunaga's lead in artistic opulence.

The completion of Osaka Castle saw it become the greatest and strongest fortress-palace in Japan. Powerful lords who visited the grand castle shortly after completion wrote that the grandiose *donjon* in the main enceinte that served as Hideyoshi's residence 'soared upwards for nine stories, nearly reaching the heavens'.[21]

Seemingly elevated to the level of a god, for Hideyoshi, who relished lavish entertainments and having power as much as he did military conquests, the 'piece de resistance' within his opulent home surely was his radiant tea room, gilded completely with gold leaf. It is here where Sen no Rikyu, arms merchant and tea master to the overlords and formerly Nobunaga's tea master, presided over parties meant to 'awe' the daimyo guests, as they often received a treasured memento of the occasion, usually a selection of fine tea utensils, all crafted from pure gold. Such mementos were a mere symbol used as a 'gift tool' in order to heighten a lord's position of power in the realm. 'To give away one of these utensils meant "awarding" a certain military commander, or entrusting power or favor onto someone. In this way the power holder gained the loyalty of his subordinates.'[22]

---

21   Atsushi Fujimoto. *Osaka-fu no Rekishi. (The History of Osaka.)* Yamakawa Publishing, Tokyo, 1969, p. 134.

22   Maria Petrucci. 'Tea Politics, Christianity, Diplomacy and the Economics of the Korean Wars: Shimai Soshitsu and Kamiya Sotan's Roles in the Process of Japan's State Formation Between 1570 and 1600.' p. 8.

A replica of Hideyoshi's famous, portable gold tea room. (Osaka Castle Museum) Taken by Katrice

Osaka Castle was an impregnable fortress, but following the balance of arms and arts in the samurai ideal. Its 'tough' exterior was matched with a gorgeous interior. Momoyama art (1573–1615) flourished during this period. It was a period of interest in the outside world, the development of large urban centers, and the rise of the merchant and leisure classes. Ornate castle architecture and interiors, adorned with painted screens embellished with gold leaf, reflected daimyo power and wealth. In fact, Azuchi-Momoyama Period (1573–1600) was named after the castles of Nobunaga and Hideyoshi![23]

> Castles were to be built large not just for defensive purposes, but to display the wealth and prestige of the lord and to impress upon his vassals and the general population of hegemon's ability to harness the material and human resources of his realm. They were also to embody refined luxury.[24]

---

[23] Momoyama was named after the hill on which Hideyoshi built his castle at Fushimi, south of Kyoto. Fushimi Castle was completed in 1594, at the end of the Sengoku Period, as Hideyohi's retirement residence.

[24] James McClain. *Osaka: The Merchants' Capital of Early Modern Japan.* Cornell University, USA, 1999, p. 12.

Upon completion, Osaka Castle was deemed a magnificent stronghold. Hideyoshi 'the warrior' used its magnificence to further acquire the prestige of the court nobility, both by its external and internal structure and decoration. The basic plan was modeled after Azuchi Castle. As mentioned earlier, Hideyoshi wanted to build a castle that mirrored Nobunaga's. In terms of artistic expression and lifestyle, Nobunaga and Hideyoshi presided over one of the most exuberant periods in all Japanese history.

CONSOLIDATION THROUGH ART

In contrast with the Zen concepts of *wabi* aesthetics, the artistic tastes of the Azuchi-Momoyama ran to the imposing, sometimes even referred to as 'gaudy', as claimed by Carolyn Wheelwright, a leading scholar of Japanese painting and architecture at Yale University. Their sumptuous castles were adorned with elaborately carved or lacquered woodwork and sliding panels and screens decorated lavishly with gold leaf and 'bold' paintings by the leading artists of the day. Consequently, Hideyoshi had now reached a point permitting indulgence in luxuries. However, in his own way, he not only became a patron of the arts but also an amateur, an enthusiast of the arts—most notably those of poetry, tea and Noh drama. His life now exemplified both arms and arts.

Birds and Flowers of the Four Seasons, c.1566, detail.
Kano Eitoku (1543-1590).
Sliding doors; ink and color on paper.
Sengoku Jidai period (1490-1573) -
Momoyama period (1573-1615).

Examples of the lavish art that decorated Hideyoshi's castle.

Cypress Trees.
Kano Eitoku (1543-1590).
Screen; ink, colors and gold leaf on paper.
Sengoku Jidai period (1490-1573) - Momoyama period (1573-1615).

Wind and Thunder Gods, detail.
Tawaraya Sotatsu (act. late 16th - early 17th century).
Screens; color, ink and gold leaf on paper.
Momoyama period (1573-1615).

Another example of the type of Momoyama art, collected by Hideyoshi, which adorned his castle's interior.

The crowning event of Hideyoshi's aristocratization was when he hosted an Imperial Visit by Emperor Go-Yozei at Juraku Palace in Kyoto on 9 May 1588. 'When Emperor Go-Yozei left his palace at noon on Tensho 16/4/14 (9 May 1588) in order to travel the fifteen short city blocks to Hideyoshi's nonesuch "Assembly of Delights," he was embarking on an elaborate spectacle indeed. Hideyoshi was a river, an ocean of magnanimity, and strove for magnificence in all things.'[25] This visit was extraordinary because it showed Hideyoshi's magnitude of power, as the emperor would often 'receive' guests and never the other way around.

Toyotomi Hideyoshi intended his Osaka Castle to become the center of a new, unified Japan under Toyotomi rule. Today too, Osaka Castle is deep-rooted in the minds of citizens of Japan as the symbol of Osaka, as is the 'Taiko' and founder of the castle, Toyotomi Hideyoshi. Osaka Castle is widely known as an emblem of the power and fortune of Toyotomi Hideyoshi. It remains the most iconic symbol of Osaka, which has been handed down through the various battles in history to the present day. This magnificent castle was reputed as being unparalleled in Japan, as was the nation's unifier and Taiko-Hideyoshi.[26]

Much like Nobunaga, Hideyoshi saw impressive structures as useful symbols of power, and so continued on a 'building program' that by his death would produce Osaka and Fushimi (or Momoyama), the latter becoming synonymous with his reign, and as the place of his death in 1598, while the first, despite being the "battlefield" of several conflicts during the unification of Japan, is considered by many Japanese people today the greatest castle ever built in Japan.

On the other hand, when Hideyoshi's Juraku Palace was completed in early 1588, rumour has it that it was 'constructed' solely to impress the emperor and 'hastily' to coincide for the occasion of the emperor's visit. It was just another impressive structure to symbolize Hideyoshi's power.

"Despite this, the emperor's visit to Juraku Palace was truly an elaborate event that marked the pinnacle of his career."

> Wheelwright gives a detailed account of the events when the emperor visited, yet simply said, the once son of a farmer and foot soldier, Hideyoshi, the one-time sandal bearer for Nobunaga, read *waka* to the emperor and treated him to a series of lavish feasts over the five day visit.[27] In addition, he made generous grants to the imperial treasury and rebuilt imperial properties.

Yet, in fact, Hideyoshi and the court shared a symbiotic relationship:

---

[25]   Wheelwright, Carolyn. 'A Visualization of Eitoku's Lost Paintings at Azuchi Castle,' in George Elison and Bardwell L. Smith (eds.), *Warlords, Artists and Commoners: Japan in the Sixteenth Century.* Hawaii University Press, 1981, p. 234.

[26]   Toyotomi resigned as *kampaku* (imperial regent) in 1591 to take the title of *taiko* (retired regent).

[27]   Waka is Japanese *tanka* poetry, consisting of only thirty one syllables, arranged in five lines of 5, 7, 5, 7, and 7 syllables, without rhyme or quantity.

Hideyoshi reinvested the court with luxury and pomp while the court provided Hideyoshi with legitimacy. Hideyoshi's governing impulse was the desire to display his wealth and his cultivation, which were incorporated in his precious tea utensils.

> Nobunaga another great aficionado of tea, had monopolized the practice of the art in his military group. The inferiors were not free to imitate the lord's accomplishment. Rather, the license to hold the tea ceremony was a cherished sign of the lord's favor; along with the presentation of tea utensils, it was issued in reward for singular loyalty.[28]

One instance of the showiness, which so affected Hideyoshi's approach to the tea ceremony, was the grand spectacle held at Kitano in Kyoto in 1587. Basically, it was a public art festival because it featured art exhibits, drama and dance performances. Moreover, Hideyoshi's tea utensils were displayed.

HIDEYOSHI REINTERPRETED

It is important to realize the many ways in which Hideyoshi changed Japanese society. In short, he was needed for Japan's modernization. He laid the foundations of three big policies that would endure the ages, existing strongly today. Those policies were: the introduction of the family registrar, the sword hunt, and the *Taiko Kenchi* (land survey).

Before Hideyoshi's rule, it was common for peasants to become warriors or even for samurai to turn to farming because of an uncertainty of no centralized government. And so upon taking control, Hideyoshi decreed that all peasants be disarmed completely. He set the basis for the Confucian social order instituted by Tokugawa Ieyasu. This forbade any non-samurai to carry weapons. The weapons were used to help create a large Buddha in Kyoto, still there today. This, in turn, provided a double pacification of the state. The image of Buddha supposedly calmed and protected the people, while the prohibition of arms ensured peace. The rightful ruler would always be the one to pacify the state. The 'Bountiful Minister' Hideyoshi *gave* peace to the country and its people. This solidified the social class system for the next three hundred years, or until Meiji and the consequent end of the samurai.

Furthermore, he ordered all Japan to be surveyed, including a census. Once this was done and all citizens were registered, he required all Japanese to stay in their respective provinces (or *han*), without official permission to go elsewhere. These steps were taken to ensure a level of peace in a period of time where samurai still roamed the countryside and peace was still new. But by surveying the countryside, Japanese land and resources could

---

28   Wheelwright, Carolyn. 'A Visualization of Eitoku's Lost Paintings at Azuchi Castle,' in George Elison and Bardwell L. Smith (eds), *Warlords, Artists and Commoners: Japan in the Sixteenth Century*. Hawaii University Press, 1981, p. 240–241.

be utilized properly. Hideyoshi sought to ensure political stability by limiting social mobility. This prevented military retainers from leaving their lords' service in order to become merchants or farmers. Similarly, it prohibited farmers from deserting their fields to become merchants or laborers. Included in this policy, the *bushi* and farmer were separated. In regards to this policy, against the farmer was called *katanagari* (刀狩り), or Sword Hunt, and against the fisherman was called *kaizoku kinshi rei* (海賊禁止令), or Fishermen's Prohibition Law. However, the rules within the policy were simple—the same for both farmer and fisherman. That is, mobility was restricted to one's own designated land area and all arms, such as swords, guns and knives, were to be 'given up', except agricultural tools.

Forbidding the lowest class from owning weapons was an effective measure to prevent peasant revolts and ensured greater stability across the land, at the expense of individual freedom. Hideyoshi, like Nobunaga, sought to solidify separations in the class structure, denying commoners weapons, while allowing them to the noble samurai class. This distinguished Japan's classes with only the samurai allowed to carry two swords. They formed Japan's top elite, and were placed at the top of society because they started an order and set a high moral example for others to follow. This system reinforced their position of power in society by justifying their ruling status.

Like Nobunaga, Hideyoshi thought there was a problem with temples and farmers having weapons, so he conducted the Great Sword Hunt in 1588 for Koya-san (Wakayama Prefecture), confiscating the farmers' weapons. With the swords he confiscated, Hideyoshi constructed the Great Buddha in *Houkouji* (方公寺) in Kyoto. This *katanagari* was part of a strict status class division.

Under Toyotomi Hideyoshi's government, the methods of rule he had inherited from Nobunaga were extended and systemized. With utmost respect, Hideyoshi had always followed the lead exhibited by his lord. 'Tokichiro did not just look up to Nobunaga as his lord and master. He became Nobunaga's apprentice, studying his master's strong points and concentrating his whole mind on the task of improving himself.'[29]

In order to enhance his own attributes and make a name for himself so as to gain ascendancy, Hideyoshi knew from the beginning he needed to continually better himself.

In 1571, Nobunaga started a survey of the agricultural lands he controlled; in 1576, he began to confiscate the weapons of the peasantry; and also standardized weights and measures. In 1579, he moved into his great castle headquarters at Azuchi. However, Nobunaga did not succeed in asserting his authority over all of Japan. Projects begun by Nobunaga were all rightfully completed by his successor, Hideyoshi—ultimately leading to Hideyoshi's main goal, which too was once Nobunaga's, country unification. To a large extent, it demonstrates that Hideyoshi followed Nobunaga's pattern for unification.

---

29   Eiji Yoshikawa. *Taiko*. Kodansha International Limited, Tokyo, 1992, p. 214. Tokichiro was the name given to Hideyoshi by Nobunaga in his early years of service.

Hideyoshi extended Nobunaga's land survey by introducing a standard measuring system called *Taiko Kenchi* (太閤検地) named after himself, Taiko Hideyoshi, by which the exact surface area size could be known. Therefore, fair and exact tax could be calculated. Coupled with a status control law called *Mibuntoseirei* (身分統制令) it allowed investigation into each family, knowing the population and the status each person held, such as samurai, farmer, artisan or merchant.

Between the twelfth and nineteenth centuries, feudal Japan had a four-tiered class system. The samurai class had the most prestige of all. Just below the samurai on the social ladder were the farmers and peasants. According to Confucian ideals, farmers were superior to artisans and merchants because they produced the food that all the other classes depended upon. Although artisans produced many beautiful and necessary goods, such as clothes, cooking utensils, and woodblock prints, they were considered less important than farmers. Even skilled samurai sword makers and boatwrights belonged to this third tier of society in feudal Japan. The artisan class lived in its own section of the major cities, segregated from the samurai (who usually lived in the daimyos' castles) and from the lower merchant class.

The bottom rung of feudal Japanese society was occupied by merchants, which included both traveling traders and shopkeepers. Merchants were often ostracized as "parasites" who profited from the labor of the more productive peasant and artisan classes. Not only did merchants live in a separate section of each city, but the higher classes were forbidden to mix with them except when conducting business.

Understanding a person's status was so important as it saw the introduction of the family registrar in Japan for the first time. It continued into the Tokugawa Period. However, tax paid then was considerably 'heavy' compared to the tax paid during the Toyotomi reign. Attributed to Hideyoshi, this land survey and 'class control' of 1591 still survives in modern Japan. Conducted annually by the local government, today it is commonly known as the population census.

CONCLUSION

Hideyoshi contributed militarily, culturally and politically to Japan. Militarily, he was a tough warrior. Culturally, he made Osaka Castle as beautiful as it was strong. Inspired by *Kinkaku-ji* in Kyoto (the Golden Pavilion), he constructed a fabulous portable tea room covered with gold leaf. Using this mobile innovation he was able to practice the tea ceremony wherever he went, powerfully projecting his unrivalled power and status. Politically, he set up a governmental system that balanced out the most powerful *daimyo*; in some ways, it could have been described as a parliament with a leader.

Upon Hideyoshi's death in 1598, Tokugawa took control, leaving in place a majority of Hideyoshi's decrees to use as a base upon which to build his own government. Through the semiotics of later rebuildings, one can sincerely notice the glorifications of Hideyoshi. It is true that Tokugawa tried to assert his power in a greater fashion by simply rebuilding Hideyoshi's castle larger in height and ground size. However, the Meiji Period was anti-Tokugawa, preferring to favor the democratic ideal of this self-made man. It is here that Hideyoshi as a modern hero has its origins. In 1931, the military's reconstruction of Hideyoshi's original castle was one of the largest displays of modern technology witnessed in Japan. It combined the power of the military with that of the enshrined warlord Toyotomi Hideyoshi, ensuring that Toyotomi's legacy remained, along with the reconstruction of his original castle, in contemporary society. The 1990s 'revival' of Osaka Castle and Hideyoshi strengthens memory, once again unifying a nation.

(三)

HIDEYOSHI AND CONTEMPORARY JAPAN: A HERO IN MODERN MEMORY

I have dreamed of a unified Japan—of a country strong and independent and modern. And now we have railroads and cannon, Western clothing. But, we cannot forget who we are or where we come from.[30]

Heroes emerge from every period in history. As countries differ through language, geography and culture, so too do their *hero* or *villain* stereotypes. Influences exist through every culture, yet true identity as defined by one's nationality, cannot be ignored nor forgotten.

THE LAST SAMURAI

When I spoke to people in Japan about Toyotomi Hideyoshi, they immediately made a connection to *The Last Samurai*. As I discovered over the course of my research, this is the image most people have of samurai. Set during a turbulent period in Japan's history as the country began its uneasy transition from ancient tradition to modern world power, it features 1870s Japan indelibly stamped with Hollywood's mark. The film is about two men from very different backgrounds who become united by honor and respect. Both are warriors who fight their demons as much as their enemies and who desire to understand and learn from each other in the hope of finding peace.

---

30   Emperor Meiji, accepting Katsumoto's sword, in *The Last Samurai*. Warner Bros. Pictures, 2003.

Tom Cruise plays Nathan Algren, a highly decorated American civil war veteran who drinks to dull the horrific war memories that haunt him. Reduced to promoting Winchester rifles, Algren is approached by Omura (Masato Harada) on behalf of the Japanese emperor who is enamoured of all things Western and willing to pay him handsomely to train his troops to quell a samurai rebellion. The task reunites Algren with an old friend (Billy Connolly) and an old enemy in Colonel Bagley (Tony Goldwyn). Despite Algren's insistence that the emperor's army is not ready to take on what Bagley dismisses as 'savages with bows and arrows', they are sent to battle the samurai led by the proud Katsumoto (Ken Watanabe). During the samurai's victory, Algren is spared when his bravery commands the attention of the stately chief. Taken back to their village, he is reluctantly nursed back to health by Taka (Koyuki), sister of Katsumoto and wife of the man Algren had killed. In the knowledge that once spring comes the emperor's troops will return, Algren is kept alive so that Katsumoto can learn about his enemy.

The two men engage in philosophical 'conversations' and come to recognize their similarities. As Katsumoto puts it, 'We are both students of war.' As Algren becomes assimilated into their way of life he notes, 'They are an intriguing people.' Contrasting with the brutal fight sequences, village life is observed in elegant detail along with the customs and values of the samurai.

After his winter with the samurai, when time comes for battle, Algren's allegiances are tested as he is faced with fighting for those who employed him or for his captors whose principles he had come to value. Then why upon watching this film in Japan, the lone *gaijin* (foreigner) in a wholly Japanese audience, did I suddenly feel somewhat isolated by the tears that were secretly, yet not silently, shed at the end of the movie? Of course I too felt a certain sadness over the end of the samurai era, but one which was not moved to tears, as I would otherwise be if it were an average Hollywood film with a reasonably sad ending. Listening to the surrounding audiences' soft sobbing and compelled to remain seated until the lights came on made me realize something about national identity. Imagined communities and narratives of identity rely heavily on history. What I had just witnessed was the linking of formal history with public culture.

1990S SAMURAI REVIVAL

Samurai and identity has been a major theme throughout twentieth century Japan. Beginning with the concept of *bushido* at the turn of the century, then with the rise of militarism in the 1930s, samurai were further exalted during the period of Japan's expansion into Asia and the Pacific War. But during the 1950s and the 1960s, interest in samurai culture in Japan waned. The unifying leaders of the past—Oda Nobunaga, Toyotomi Hideyoshi, Tokugawa Ieyasu, and even Sakamoto Ryoma (a hero for his contribution to the Meiji Restoration)—were seen principally as heroes of management, as Japan built itself out of the rubble into an economic dynamo. During the 1960s and 1970s, films differed far from the samurai ideal. Since the defeat in the Pacific, a new theme of freedom began. Films were simple, joyous and peaceful. But after the 'bubble economy' Japan witnessed in the 1980s, the economic downturn of the 1990s left many citizens disillusioned and longing for the spiritual, rather than the material Japan.

Akira Kurosawa's 1954 film, *Seven Samurai*, was one of the first great samurai movies to grace the screen. In 1990 at the age of eighty, Japan's most widely admired film director, Akira Kurosawa, was awarded an honorary Oscar at the Academy Awards in Hollywood. From the latter half of the 1940s until his death in 1998, Kurosawa had directed over thirty films including *Rashomon* (1950), *Seven Samurai* (1954), *Throne of Blood* (1957), and *Ran* (1976). He directed samurai epics, crime thrillers, literary adaptations, and films of social realism. One film, *Seven Samurai*, set during the *sengoku jidai*, is thought by many to be the greatest Japanese film of all time. His work had a huge influence on directors like George Lucas and Steven Spielberg who revered him as 'Master of the Cinema'. When he died on September 6, 1998, Spielberg called him 'the pictorial Shakespeare of our time'. However, he was criticized in Japan for appealing to an international audience, yet he did more than anyone else to reveal Japanese society to the West.

KUROSAWA'S CONTRIBUTION

Born in 1910, Kurosawa's career spanned the most dramatic century in Japan's history and saw its transformation from a semi-feudal empire into an industrial superstate. Kurosawa was born into a samurai family, and therefore found it easier to write about samurai. Still, he was considered by his strict father as 'falling out of his class' because he chose a career in film. Initially writing propaganda war stories, Kurosawa made his first film in 1943. During World War II, it was difficult to get scripts filmed, yet he knew his first film *Sugata Sanshiro* would immediately appeal to the military because of its directness, austerity, and athletic beauty.

Freedom and democracy of the post-war era were seen as the new ideals of freedom in Japan and national policy and war-time censoring meant that certain contents had to be included. Despite this censorship and the new post-war ideals, *Seven Samurai*, now acclaimed by Japanese as Kurosawa's greatest film, was released in 1954. Soon after this, he elevated the cliché-filled samurai swordfight movie to an art form. 'Viewers gain a deep appreciation of how rigid the class divisions used to be, and the extraordinary mental and physical alertness of the best samurai.'[31] He wanted to present the past as meaningful to the Japanese within the framework of a *jidai-geki* (period film).

In *Seven Samurai*, we have a particularly impressive example, however, because, since it is a historical film, we can see more clearly, we can see freshly. We have become so used to our own epoch that we don't even see it any more. We are blind to it. The period of civil wars, the presumably exotic and distant sixteenth century, however—that is another matter. Things become clear and in a way the problem becomes simpler, Kurosawa

---

31   Mark Weston. *Giants of Japan*. Kodansha International Limited, Tokyo, New York, London, 1999, p. 314.

may go further in his explorations than he has done before. He can, as it were, go beyond reality and try to find what is there.[32]

It is set in the war-ravaged sixteenth century and begins when farmers learn that their village is about to be raided by forty bandits on horseback. To protect their women and crops, the farmers decide to hire samurai to defend them. The same as the battle scenes we witness in *The Last Samurai*, that is horses galloping, mud flying, close-ups of pounding hooves, and dying men falling off their horses, the slow motion death is a cliché today, but its origin is credited to this much earlier released film.

Seven Samurai was a box office success both in Japan and abroad and won the Academy Award for best Foreign Film in 1955. Akira Kurosawa was a maker of films. Films were his true medium. 'Unlike real-life, it is difficult to avoid honesty in film,' he once said.

This was how Akira Kurosawa lived his life.

2003 and 1954 classic samurai films.

32   Donald Richie. *The Films of Akira Kurosawa*. University of California Press, Berkeley, Los Angeles, London, 1984, p. 98.

Manga and Television

As a result of the American occupation, post-war Japan and its censorship laws for cinema were very strict. This gave way for an even bigger 'boom' in Japan—*manga*. Artists found that portrayal of important historical events could well define a nation in just the same way as film, yet in 'print with comics'. Manga became mainstream in Japan during the US occupation, which started at the end of World War II and lasted until 1952. Japanese artists inspired by US comics, like Disney and Betty Boop, decided to create their own in a distinct style. These increasingly began to appear in newspapers and magazines as comic strips. Graphically, the blank page was the artist's canvas, his battlefield if you like, and depictions of images were seldom censored, only those of a pornographic nature (which were rare) or inappropriate accompanied text. The new ideal of freedom, it seemed, was expressed and flowed easier in comics and criticism was significantly lesser. Furthermore, besides being sometimes educational, comics were welcomed and appreciated by everyone. Children and adults of all ages today still enjoy reading *manga*.

Besides changing Japanese institutions, the Americans wanted the Japanese people to better understand the idea of democracy. To do this, the occupation government used its control of newspaper, magazine, radio and cinema to explain and popularize democracy. Perhaps they offered a lighter insight to an abstract reality that one could only imagine, especially in the time of the samurai.

By the mid-1960s, television viewing had reduced the size of movie audiences and studios were more cautious about authorizing films with big budgets or unorthodox themes. Finally, audiences could tune in from the comfort of their own home to watch historical masterpieces. More than sixty years later, historical epics still rank highly on the national order of 'most viewed programs' in Japanese households.

Various manga depictions of the Sengoku Period.

Kampaku Hideyoshi

**The three unifiers
From the top – Nobunaga
Hideyoshi, Tokugawa**

**Hideyoshi avenging
Nobunaga's death in 1582.**

Battle flags of feudal lords.

The 'fury' of samurai battle.

In 1996, Hideyoshi had never been more popular. He was the subject of numerous magazine publications—both educational and adult- centered, comic books, exhibitions and a mini-series, otherwise known as a 'Taiga drama' (大河ドラマ). In Japan, the New Year means a new 'Taiga drama'. Every Sunday night at 8:00 p.m., NHK (national channel, no commercials) broadcasts its large scale 'Taiga drama'. The word *taiga* means 'great river' in English. Appropriately, it is suggestive of the epic nature of the programs. Broadcasts of the dramas began in 1963, just ten years after the start of national broadcasting in Japan. NHK's 'Taiga drama' is a cultural institution, a year-long serial about an important figure in Japanese history. Since 1963, over sixty titles have aired already. The intention was to portray history in a way that could compete with the cinema. Themed around historical figures or events, these long-running dramas showcase the story of the protagonist(s) and what the world was like back when they were alive, as well as how they interacted with those around them. One distinct characteristic of any taiga drama is its large scale, with a grand cast, gorgeous and colourful outfits, and gigantic filming sets and locations. These locations alone gather huge public interest annually and attract enormous numbers of tourists and "fan -following". Since care is put into ensuring faithful depiction of the historical setting, people and events, taiga dramas are very enjoyable for all ages while also learning more about their Japanese history. With some fifty installments of forty five minutes, there are nearly forty hours in every serial.

Many of the serials focus on leading historical figures, such as the brutal yet clever Oda Nobunaga and big success story of Toyotomi Hideyoshi, which aired in 1996. Historical drama is central to the construction of national identity, for our understanding of the world is shaped by stories. In this sense, the 'Taiga dramas' are an affirmation of what it is to be Japanese these days. Given the prestige of NHK, they represent the establishment's view of the past and the lessons that should be drawn. More than most programs, they offer a window into the national soul. In the case of Hideyoshi, it reveals the importance of having ambitions and working hard to achieve success.

秀吉

NHK大河ドラマ・ストーリー

後篇

衛星第2夜10時30分放送

NHK総合テレビ夜8時放送

放送＝毎週日曜日

原作＝堺屋太一

脚本＝竹山洋

協力＝NHKドラマ制作班

1996 NHK Taiga Drama, "Hideyoshi". (Naoto Takenaka)

The locations used for the historical series usually induce those communities to organize events based on the dramas to attract tourists. In 1996, *Hideyoshi* was no exception. The leading character of Toyotomi Hideyoshi was played by Naoto Takenaka. This alone attracted television audiences as Naoto was considered a 'good' actor, as well as being handsome and strong. The story was simple, a classic success story about none other than Toyotomi Hideyoshi (1537–1598), the military ruler who succeeded in uniting Japan during the Sengoku Period. Amongst the warlords of this period, Hideyoshi is certainly one of Japan's most popular figures, particularly in the *Kansai* (Osaka) region. In 1996 when Hideyoshi became 'popular again', many events took place, especially in the *Kansai* area. One such Hideyoshi related event that stood out was the *Hideyoshi Tenkaichi* Festival in Himeji, which was counting on the success of the event to help it overcome the wounds of the Great Hanshin Earthquake that happened on January 17, 1995.

HIDEYOSHI CONNECTION: A CATALYST FOR RECOVERY

The link between the city and Hideyoshi is Himeji Castle, also known as *Shirasagi-jyo* (White Heron Castle) for its elegant form reminiscent of a snowy heron spreading its wings in flight. Himeji Castle is a national treasure of Japan and was added to UNESCO's World Heritage list in 1993. A first-class tourist attraction, the castle received an average of 900,000 visitors annually until 1994, when its World Heritage listing brought the number up to 1.2 million, including a marked increase in foreign visitors.

However, because of the devastating earthquake in January 1995, the number of visitors that year dropped to just 60 percent of the annual average. This is where Hideyoshi helped the city's recovery. When Nobunaga was striving to unite Japan in the latter part of the sixteenth century, Hideyoshi was ordered to subjugate Mori Terumoto, the then lord of the *Chugoku* region. Making Himeji Castle his base, Hideyoshi first conquered Harima (Hyogo Prefecture) before attacking Takamatsu Castle in Bitchu (Okayama Prefecture). It was here that Hideyoshi heard the news of Nobunaga's defeat at Honnoji Temple in Kyoto. 'With a force of 20,000 men, Hideyoshi turned back and made the 210 kilometer journey to Yamazaki, Kyoto, in just five days, a breathtaking achievement in that era.'[33] This feat came to be known as 'The Great Chugoku Reversal', and it opened the way for Hideyoshi to become the ruler of a united Japan.

These historical events form the basis for Himeji's claim that Himeji Castle was the starting point of Hideyoshi's campaign to rule the entire country. Therefore, in 1996, Himeji held some fifty events under the theme of this popular ruler and his ties to Himeji. The main event was the NHK taiga drama 'Hideyoshi and Himeji'. For three days, there was also a re-enactment of 'The Great Chugoku Reversal'. Other Hideyoshi related events included an armor and weapons exhibition of the period, a castle seminar where guests could learn

---

33   'Kansai Window' in *Kippo News*. Volume 3. No. 91. (Tuesday, June 4, 1996.)

all about Himeji Castle, a pottery fair, and tea ceremony demonstrations. Head of Himeji's tourism promotions section, Mr. Kiyoshi Matsumoto said, 'We want to use Hideyoshi as a catalyst to recover from the earthquake and revitalize the local economy. This is also an opportunity for people both here and throughout the country to learn about Himeji's history.'[34]

34   'Kansai Window' in *Kippo News*. Volume 3. No. 91. (Tuesday, June 4, 1996.)

Heisei-restored Osaka Castle.

Present day Himeji Castle.
Its structure exceeds that of Osaka Castle
but remains much smaller in comparison to Osaka Castle's ground size.

THE JAPANESE WARRIOR HERO

They say Japan was made by a sword. They say the old gods dipped a coral blade into the ocean and when they pulled it out, four perfect drops fell back into the sea and those drops became the islands of Japan. I say Japan was made by a handful of brave men. Warriors willing to give their lives for what seems to have become a forgotten word: *Honor.*[35]

The ancient medieval war tales of Japan have celebrated the warrior hero as the ideal to which those who serve the *shogunate* strive. However, the picture they paint is somewhat different than popular Western perceptions and stereotypes suggest. Samurai movies usually depict a *daimyo* with only a single sword by which to punish 'criminals' and their band of subordinates in a brutal yet seemingly effortless fashion.

Samurai employed a range of weapons such as bows and arrows, spears and guns. But their most famous weapon and their symbol was the sword. Samurai were supposed to lead their lives according to the ethical code of *bushido* ('the way of the warrior'). Strongly Confucian in nature, *bushido* stressed concepts such as loyalty to one's master, self-discipline and respectful, ethical behavior. 'His armor, weapons, demeanor, his whole style of life, separated the samurai from the rest of society. The typical samurai was a figure on horseback armed with bow and sword.'[36]

These great country associates remain modern day heroes, and despite how very diverse they are, they all have one thing in common. That is, they all began from a pedigree line or were born into 'greatness'. Not anyone could become a warrior, it needed to be 'in the blood'. In the case of the hero of this story, Hideyoshi had neither direct claim to samurai ancestry nor the status of a pedigree lineage. The success story of Hideyoshi is one which will never again be repeated in history. He remains a popular figure because of who he was, a respected, self-made man who worked hard to reach the heights of greatness. I believe it is for this reason that his fans 'made' him a modern hero.

A classic source written in English about the ancient samurai is Dr. Paul Varley's book, *Warriors of Japan.* According to Varley, although the sword, *katana,* was definitely the symbol of the warrior class in the age of the shogunal restoration under the Tokugawa, mounted warriors on horseback, with the bow and arrow as their weapon of choice, were considered the elite warriors in early medieval times. Lesser warriors, however, such as the foot soldier, often made use of spears and were seldom depicted fighting with a bow and arrow. Later, in the *Sengoku* Period, foot soldiers used the bow and arrow, but since the introduction of firearms, this made the weapon nearly obsolete. This announced the end of the idealistic heroes of the medieval period and the consequent introduction of the science of warfare.

---

[35] Simon Graham, the British 'old Japan hand' and interpreter (perhaps inspired by Basil Hall Chamberlain) in *The Last Samurai.* Warner Bros. Pictures, 2003. Directed by Edward Zwick.

[36] Richard Storry and Werner Forman. *The Way of the Samurai.* Orbis Publishing Limited, London, 1978, p. 41.

A classic early 'warrior' image of Hideyoshi.

So, what makes a hero? The Oxford Dictionary defines a hero as 'a person noted or admired for nobility, courage, outstanding achievements, etc.' Expectedly, heroes emerge from every period in history. Another hero, which emerged from early Japan was the *kamikaze*. This term became largely associated with the Japanese suicide-fighter pilots during World War II. However, it originated many centuries before. In 1274, the Mongols invaded Japan via Korea in the great military campaign of Genghis Khan. Encountering an unprecedented array of technologically advanced weapons, such as grenade-type explosives and catapults, the Japanese suffered many losses in just one day. However, because it was monsoon season in this area of Asia, a storm arose and the Mongols' boats were obliterated. Following this in 1281, the Mongols sent a much larger army to Japan, but once again they were repelled by yet another one of these 'natural disasters'. These storms were called *kamikaze* (lit. God winds). These *kamikaze* were viewed by the Japanese as unmistakable proof that the gods had favored and protected them in their time of need.

Centuries later in the 'modern world', this term became synonymous with World War II Japanese suicide-fighter pilots and still remains as the image of *kamikaze* today, as I discovered when asking some Australians what they knew of *kamikaze*. These suicide-fighter pilots were called *kamikaze* for they would, in effect, become the winds sent down from the gods to destroy their enemy.

COLLECTIVE MEMORY AND PUBLIC CULTURE: INVENTING, FORGETTING, REMEMBERING

'Collective memory' exists among groups of people who have shared experiences and wish to remember them. Collective memory is a valid, living entity. Takashi Fujitani, professor of history at the University of California San Diego discusses the concept of cultural history to inspire nationalism. In his book, *Splendid Monarchy*, Fujitani illustrates what visual symbols and rituals reveal about monarchy, nationalism, discipline, gender, memory and modernity by using ceremonials such as imperial weddings and funerals as models. Focusing on the Meiji Period (1868–1912), the period in which *The Last Samurai* was set, Fujitani brings recent methods of cultural history to a study of modern Japanese nationalism for the first time. The opening chapter, entitled 'Inventing, Forgetting, Remembering', shows how much of what we now accept as long-standing Japanese tradition has its origins in the efforts of Meiji leaders to create a sense of shared citizenship in the newly created state. Most people think that the emperor of Japan has been a lasting symbol from the 'start' of Japan, which is very wrong. After the success of the Meiji Restoration, they made all the customs including such things as weddings and images of the emperor. From 'inventing' all these things, they could easily plant into the people's mind that the emperor has been there, watching 'his' people from the beginning of the country. Takashi Fujitani demonstrates that this is the foundation of Japanese nationalism, giving a fascinating and detailed account of the invention of the modern Japanese state through displays of imperial power and pageantry.

Rather than 'forgetting' the events that shaped the country of Japan, Fujitani proposes that we remember in order to illuminate the culture/power nexus in modern Japan. This was also evident in *The Last Samurai* when Emperor Meiji accepted Katsumoto's sword. His point is that remembering and forgetting are linked in the process of 'selective remembering'. He in turn explores how a consideration of space and place can contribute to theoretical concerns such as identity, globalization, nationalism and gender.

Before Hideyoshi's reign and through the Edo Period, Japan was populated by a people separated from one another regionally, with strong local, rather than national ties. For example, showing loyalty to one's domain lord. In what Fujitani calls *mnemonic sites*, or official signs or symbols, was the rulers' attempt to involve the common people in a selected culture of a national community. Since Meiji and the installment of the emperor, the citizens of Japan expressed a new, more common loyalty. Fujitani also discusses an example of one dominant memory used to unite the people of Japan —the invention of national holidays.

According to Fujitani, the creation of mnemonic sites creates a culture of nationalism. Or, simply put, symbols, including reproductions of visuals in places such as school textbooks, are used to create memory. In exactly the same way as Toyotomi Hideyoshi exists in contemporary society, statues, monuments, and the enshrined, serve as powerful mnemonic sites in Japan today to remind us of our 'heroes'. As mentioned in part one, Emperor Meiji himself enshrined Hideyoshi.

A HERO IN MODERN MEMORY

As largely as he once did, Hideyoshi still exists in Japan today. School textbooks remind students of the importance of this figure and of the great effect he had on society. The study of a Japanese junior high school history textbook can really help to understand what the Japanese government considers 'important' in the way of history education for students. The focus I think is more on the visual rather than the textual. Perhaps this is to emphasise the arts and culture adored by Hideyoshi— beautiful, tranquil gardens, precious pottery, and exquisite artworks by the leading artists of the day.

Encompassing the aspect of power, definitely what I consider to be the theme of the *Sengoku* Period, is the notable amount of space dedicated to Hideyoshi in textbooks. Compared to the other two unifiers, Nobunaga and Tokugawa, Hideyoshi's 'space' is marginally larger, a possible display of power. Lacking mention of his invented lineage, he appears to be 'heroized' in school textbook print surrounded by his powerful and great achievements in both politics and battle.

Competing for power in the Sengoku Period, a period in Japanese history consumed with almost-constant civil war, social upheaval, and political intrigue for over a century, saw Hideyoshi remain as the most truly glorified unifier in a scholastic context. The period is undoubtedly consumed with battle, war, and culture. However, Hideyoshi remains undeniably glorified in an educational sense.

HIDEYOSHI'S MNEMONIC SITES

Shortly after his death, Toyotomi Hideyoshi was deified in the magnificent Toyokuni Jinja Shrine. The original shrine was destroyed by Tokugawa Ieyasu, who overthrew the Toyotomi clan, and so the shrine standing today was rebuilt in 1880, a mnemonic site since Meiji. The peace he had brought to Japan had held together out of personal loyalties that ran deep, for Hideyoshi had amassed tremendous wealth and lavished it on the imperial court and on various lords throughout the country (hence his posthumous title, Toyokuni).

Finally, Hideyoshi was enshrined in his own temple called Toyokuni ('Wealth of the Nation') sitting above the Great Buddha he had built in Kyoto so, like a god, to continue 'watching' over his people. His shrine became and remains a popular Shinto site.

Mnemonic sites may exist illustrated with text also. Herbert Plutschow's *Historical Kyoto* is a tourist guidebook, useful in listing the mnemonic sites—the standard tourist itinerary, complete with retelling of the mythology. It introduces the history of Kyoto from the Heian Period (794–1185) to the Meiji Period (1868–1912) with the historical spots or the sites that are associated with historical figures in each era. Simply written and beautifully illustrated, the many pages entailing Hideyoshi give not an historical overview of his greatness, as most other sources do, as much as they give a detailed description of Hideyoshi's cultural life.

豊国神社

―参拝のしおり―

Kampaku Hideyoshi charms the cover of this modern pamphlet guide to Toyokuni Shrine.
Taken by Katrice.

Beginning with the reconstruction of Kyoto under Hideyoshi, of streets and temple wards, fortification and city gates, the shift moves to his adornment of all things great—the construction of the Great Buddha and his Fushimi Castle. From Plutschow, one can learn about cultural life under Hideyoshi, from the paintings he chose to his love for poetry, Noh drama, and the tea ceremony.

Plutschow artistically concludes the end of Hideyoshi's era and his demise not with policies, but with enshrinement at Toyokuni Shrine and Kodai-ji Temple. Respectively, these are the gravesites of Hideyoshi and his wife 'Ne-ne'. Plutschow's book is a primary resource about a warrior who became 'cultured'.

As Fujitani mentions of mnemonic sites that help one to remember history and events of another time, these fall not short with our hero. Hideyoshi has even been popularized by the renowned Sony Playstation, Nintendo and Xbox gaming consoles worldwide, on the battlefield along with Nobunaga! The annual Nagoya Festival still parades all the unifiers along the main street on horseback in a grand spectacle for all to see and 'remember'. Millions of visitors annually visit Osaka and Himeji Castles, remaining national treasures for the people of Japan.

Conclusion

Toyotomi Hideyoshi was truly a remarkable figure, an anomalous character in the pageant of Japanese history. Few Japanese leaders have attracted as much adulation and hero worship from both scholars and the general public, to the extent that Hideyoshi is recreated. Eiji Yoshikawa, in his famous book *Taiko*, which has been both a consequence of the twentieth century interest in Hideyoshi and part of its enshrinement, presents Hideyoshi in a role of an infallible metaphor for the author's idealized version of Japan itself.

Mary Berry's 1982 biography *Hideyoshi* sifts through Hideyoshi's career, attempting to place his ideas and activities in a manner compatible with modern assumptions regarding developments in Japanese history.

Modern Japanese television dramas, *manga*, video games and novels continue to popularize Hideyoshi's life, updated of course to account for modern social standards.

Hideyoshi is often portrayed as a hero, a shining figure and the progenitor of a golden age. I believe he deserves much of his acclaim, as he embodied the spirit of his age, and as fate would have it, was the one to bring it to a close. His policies and initiatives made the Tokugawa shogunate possible, shaping and changing Japanese history in ways still discernible today.

A common parable, known widely in Japan, illustrastes the different personalities of each of these three most powerful warlords of the Sengoku Period.

What would they each do if a cuckoo didn't sing?

> *'If you don't sing, I'll kill you,'* Nobunaga said.
> *'If you don't sing, I'll make you sing,'* Hideyoshi said.
> *'If you don't sing, I'll wait until you sing,'* Tokugawa said.

The man who made the cuckoo want to sing, Toyotomi Hideyoshi looms large in the memory of Japanese history - larger perhaps than any man before or since.

Modern day Osaka Castle.

Manga depiction of a truly satisfied Kampaku Hideyoshi,
after having the title of *Kampaku* bestowed upon him by the emperor in 1585.
Hideyoshi was forty nine years old.

A classic *manga* as depicted in Eiji Yoshikawa's epic novel *Taiko*.
This skillfully drawn battle scene alone heroizes Hideyoshi,
as seen in the center with his magnificent castle behind him.

CONCLUSION

A great man is not made simply by his innate ability. Circumstances must give him the opportunity. These circumstances are often the malevolent conditions that surround a man and work on his character, almost as if they were trying to torture him. When his enemies have taken every form possible, both seen and unseen, and ally themselves to confront him with every hardship imaginable, he encounters the real test of greatness.[37]

Toyotomi Hideyoshi was truly a remarkable figure in the pageant of Japanese history. Few other Japanese leaders have attracted as much adulation and hero worship from both scholars and the general public, to the extent that Hideyoshi is recreated, it seems, every few decades in a new, even more relevant image. Oda Nobunaga had attempted to unify Japan through sheer brute force; Toyotomi furthered this endeavor by concentrating on the arts of peace and administration. Nobunaga had done, you might say, all the 'dirty work' and it was left to Toyotomi to forge a new administrative organization to guarantee unification. The government that he built was founded on the old feudal system of personal loyalties rather than administrative centrality. While he pacified the country, he did not fundamentally change the Japanese way of national life. Most of the measures that Hideyoshi employed would become the basis of Tokugawa rule only a decade later and were instrumental in the long period of quiet that characterized the Tokugawa Period (1603–1868). Foremost among these were Hideyoshi's laws barring social mobility. He was concerned about people like himself, who had risen from obscurity through the force of ambition and ruthless single-mindedness. Hideyoshi made class a permanent status for individuals and their offspring; in particular, he made the samurai, who were the professional soldiers of Japan, into a separate class and forbade anyone from the non-samurai class to carry weapons or armor, consequently terminating civil bloodshed.

By his death in September 1598, Hideyoshi had lived a lifetime of war. This individual changed the course of history. His achievements were immense, probably the greatest ever by any Japanese leader in history. He had

---

37   Eiji Yoshikawa. *Taiko*. Kodansha International Limited, Tokyo, 1992, pp. 338–9.

brought peace, unified the country, ended the civil wars and had created what seemed to be political equilibrium amongst Japan's most powerful daimyos.

Beginning in the most obscure circumstances, Hideyoshi's rise is an astonishing triumph over one's humble origins, from the son of a peasant farmer to the undisputed and unrivaled leader of a unified Japan by 1590. Undeniably, Toyotomi Hideyoshi made a lasting legacy for himself as truly one of the greatest Japanese modern heroes in both history and memory.

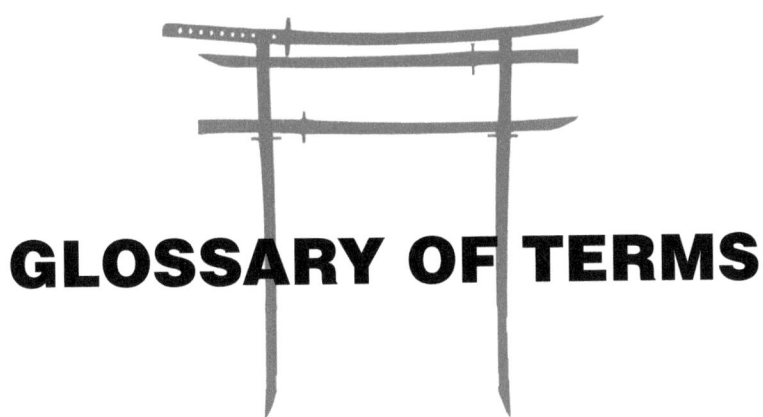

GLOSSARY OF TERMS

Ashigaru—Foot soldier

Bakufu—Shogun's government

Bushi—Samurai warrior

Bushido—The way of the warrior (ethical code of the samurai)

Daimyo—Feudal lord

Kampaku—Imperial regent

Manga—Japanese for comics

Sengoku Jidai—The warring-states period

Seppuku—Suicide by disembowelment

Shugo—Military governor

Shogun—Great general

Taiko—Retired imperial regent

Wabi—Enjoyment of a humble, simple, quiet and contemplative state of mind (Zen Buddhism origins)

BIBLIOGRAPHY

Allen, Jeanne. *Designer's Guide to Samurai Patterns.* Chronicle Books, San Francisco, 1990.

Barker, Philip. *Michel Foucault.* Edinburgh University Press, Edinburgh, 1998.

Beardsley, Hall, Ward. *Village Japan.* The University of Chicago Press, 1959.

Berry, Mary Elizabeth. *Hideyoshi.* Harvard University Press, Cambridge (Massachusetts) and London, 1982.

Berry, Mary E. 'Chapter 7: The Freedom of Invention', in *The Culture of Civil War in Kyoto.* University of California Press, California, 1994 (Pp. 242–284).

Bito, Masahide and Watanabe, Akio. *A Chronological Outline of Japanese History.* International Society for Educational Information, Inc., Tokyo.

Boscaro, Adriana. *101 Letters of Hideyoshi.* The Kawata Press, Tokyo, 1975.

Bryan, J. Ingram. *The Civilization of Japan.* Thornton Butterworth Limited, London, 1927.

Carr, Edward. *What is History?* Macmillan, London, 1961.

Coaldrake, William H. 'The Changing Countenances of Aristocratic and Warrior Power' and 'The Symbol and Substance of Momoyama and Early Edo Authority', in *Architecture and Authority in Japan.* Routledge, London, 1996 (Pp. 81–138).

Collcutt, Martin and Jansen, M. (Eds.) *Cultural Atlas of Japan.* New York, 1988.

Cooper, Michael (Trans.). 'Chapter 33: The General Way in which the Japanese Entertain with Cha', in *Joao Rodrigues's Account of Sixteenth Century Japan.* Kodansha International Limited, Tokyo, New York, 1973 (Pp. 263–286).

Cooper, Michael (ed.). *They Came To Japan: An Anthology of European Reports on Japan 1543–1640*. University of California Press, Berkeley and Los Angeles, 1965.

Danaher, Geoff; Schirato, Tony and Webb, Jen. *Understanding Foucault*. Allen & Unwin, Sydney, 2000.

Duus, Peter. *The Rise of Modern Japan*. Houghton Mifflin Co., Stanford University, 1976.

Elison George. 'Hideyoshi, The Bountiful Minister', in G. Elison and B. L. Smith, eds., *Warlords, Artists and Commoners*. University Press of Hawaii, 1981. (Pp. 223–244).

Fujiki Hisashi with George Elison, 'The Political Posture of Oda Nobunaga', in John Whitney Hall et al. (eds.), *Japan Before Tokugawa: Political Consolidation and Economic Growth, 1500– 1650*. Princeton University Press, New Jersey, 1981.

Fujitani, Takashi. 'Chapter One: Inventing, Forgetting, Remembering', in *Splendid Monarchy* (Pp. 1–28). University of California Press, 1996.

Gluck, Jay. *Zen Combat*. Weatherhill, New York, 1996.

Gordon, Colin. *Power/Knowledge: Selected Interviews and Other Writings, 1972–1977*. Harvester Press Ltd, 1980.

Guth, Christine. *Art, Tea and Industry: Masuda Takashi and the Mitsui Circle*. Princeton University Press, New Jersey, 1993.

Hall, John Whitney. 'Bizen and the Sengoku Daimyo' and 'Nobunaga, Hideyoshi, and the Unification of the Daimyo', in *Government and Local Power in Japan 500–1700*. Princeton University Press, New Jersey, 1966 (Pp. 238–295).

Hall, John Whitney. 'Hideyoshi's Domestic Policies', in J. W. Hall, K. Nagahara and K. Yamamura, eds., *Japan Before Tokugawa: Political Consolidation and Economic Growth, 1500–1650*. Princeton University Press, Princeton, 1981. (Pp. 194–223).

Hall, John W. and Beardsley, Richard K. *Twelve Doors to Japan*. McGraw-Hill Book Company, U.S.A., 1965.

Hall, John W. and Mass, Jeffrey P. *Medieval Japan*. Stanford University Press, California, 1974.

Hane, Mikiso. *Premodern Japan*. Westview Press, Boulder, 1991.

Hinaga, Motoo. (Translated by William H. Coaldrake) *Japanese Castles*. Kodansha International Limited, 1986.

Hogan, Michael J. *Hiroshima in History and Memory*. Cambridge University Press, 1996.

Hurley, Robert (Trans.) Foucault, Michel. *Aesthetics. The Essential Works 2*. Allen Lane. The Penguin Press, 1998.

Ikegami, Eiko. *The Taming of the Samurai*. Harvard University Press, Cambridge, 1995.

Jansen, Marius B. *Warrior Rule in Japan*. Cambridge University Press, 1995.

Japan. Profile of a Nation. Kodansha International, Tokyo, 1995. Latourette, Kenneth Scott. *History of Japan*. Macmillan, New York, 1957.

Lu, David John. *Sources of Japanese History*. McGraw-Hill, 1974.

Mason, R. and Caiger, J. *A History of Japan*. Tuttle Company, Tokyo, 1972.

Mass, Jeffrey P. *Antiquity and Anachronism in Japanese History*. Stanford University Press, New Jersey, 1985.

McClain, James and Wakita, Osamu. *Osaka. The Merchants' Capital of Early Modern Japan*. Cornell University Press, Ithaca and London, 1999.

Merquior, J. G. *Foucault*. Fontana Press, 1985.

Morris, Dixon. 'The City of Sakai and Urban Autonomy', in G. Elison and B. L. Smith, eds., *Warlords, Artists and Commoners*. University Press of Hawaii, 1981 (Pp. 23–54).

Morton, Scott W. *Japan, Its History and Culture*. Wren Publishing Pty Ltd., Melbourne, 1973.

Murakami, Hyoe and Harper, Thomas J. *Great Historical Figures of Japan*. Japan Cultural Institute, Tokyo, 1978.

Nakane, Chie. *Japanese Society*. University of California Press, California, 1970.

Nakane, Chie and Oishi, Shinzaburo. 'The Bakuhan System', in *Tokugawa Japan*. University of Tokyo Press, 1990 (Pp. 11–37).

Newman, John. *Bushido. The Way of the Warrior*. Bison Books, London, 1989.

Nish, Ian. *The Story of Japan*. Faber and Faber, London, 1968.

Ooms, Herman. *Tokugawa Ideology. Early Constructs, 1570–1680*. Princeton University Press, Princeton, 1985.

Petrucci, Maria. 'Tea Politics, Christianity, Diplomacy and the Economics of the Korean Wars: Shimai Soshitsu and Kamiya Sotan's Roles in the Process of Japan's State Formation Between 1570 and 1600.' A paper presented at the Graduate Student Research Conference; Asia Pacific: Local Knowledge Versus Western Theory. Hosted by the Institute of Asian Research and the Center for Japanese Research, The University of British Columbia, February 5–7, 2004.

Plutschow, Herbert. *Historical Kyoto.* The Japan Times Limited, 1983.

Plutschow, Herbert and Keene, Donald. *Introducing Kyoto.* Kodansha International Limited, Tokyo, 1979.

Rabinow, Paul. *The Foucault Reader.* Pantheon Books, New York, 1984.

Reischauer, Edwin O. and Craig, Albert M. *Japan: Tradition and Transformation.* Allen and Unwin, Sydney, 1989.

Richie, Donald. 'Shichinin no Samurai', in *The Films of Akira Kurosawa.* University of California Press, Berkeley, Los Angeles, London, 1984 (Pp. 97–108).

Said, Edward. *Orientalism.* Penguin Books Limited, London, 1978.

Saito, Hisho. (Translated by Elizabeth Lee and Paul Kegan) *A History of Japan.* Trench, Trubner and Co., Ltd., London, 1912.

Sheridan, Alan (Trans.) Foucault, Michel. *Discipline and Punish. The Birth of the Prison.* Vintage Books, 1979.

Sheridan, Alan (Trans.) Foucault, Michel. *The Will to Truth.* Tavistock Publications, London and New York, 1980.

Smith, Bardwell L. 'Japanese Society and Culture in the Momoyama Era: A Bibliographic Essay', in George Elison and Bardwell L. Smith (eds.), *Warlords, Artists and Commoners: Japan in the Sixteenth Century.* Hawaii University Press, 1981 (Pp. 245–280).

Soshitsu, Sen XV. *Tea Life, Tea Mind.* (trans. and ed. In the Foreign Affairs Section, Urasenke Foundation, Kyoto, Japan) Weatherhill Inc., Tokyo, New York, 1979.

Storry, Richard. *The Way of the Samurai.* Orbis Publishing Limited, London, 1978.

Taylor, Chris; Goncharoff, Nicko; Florence, Mason; Rowthorn, Christian. *Japan.* Lonely Planet Publications, Hawthorn, Australia, 1997.

Totman, Conrad. *Japan Before Perry*. University of California Press, Berkeley, 1981.

Tsunoda, Theodore de Bary, Keene. 'Chapter XV: Heroes and Hero Worship', in *Sources of Japanese Tradition Vol. 1*. Colombia University Press, New York and London, 1958 (Pp. 298–335).

Ueda, Makoto. *Matsuo Basho*. Kodansha International, Tokyo, New York, London, 1982.

Varley, Paul. *Japanese Culture*. Tuttle, Tokyo, 1990.

Varley, Paul. 'The Culture of Tea: From Its Origins to Sen no Rikyu', in George Elison and Bardwell L. Smith (eds.), *Warlords, Artists and Commoners: Japan in the Sixteenth Century*. Hawaii University Press, 1981 (Pp. 187–222).

Varley, Paul. 'The Tale of the Heike. The Warriors End', in *Warriors of Japan As Portrayed in the War Tales*. University of Hawaii Press, Honolulu, 1994 (Pp. 101–125).

Varley, Paul and Kamakura, Isao. *Tea and Japan: Essays on the History of Chanoyu*. University of Hawaii Press, Honolulu, 1989.

Weston, Mark. *Giants of Japan*. Kodansha International, New York, Tokyo, London, 1999.

Wheelwright, Carolyn. 'A Visualization of Eitoku's Lost Paintings at Azuchi Castle', in George Elison and Bardwell L. Smith (eds.), *Warlords, Artists and Commoners: Japan in the Sixteenth Century*. Hawaii University Press, 1981 (Pp. 87–113).

Wright, Tom and Mizuno, Katsuhiko. *Zen Gardens*. Mitsumura Suiko Shoin Co. Ltd., Kyoto, 1990.

Yamamoto, Tsunetomo (Trans. By William Scott Wilson). *Hagakure*. Kodansha International, Tokyo, New York, London, 1983.

Yamamura, Kozo, ed. *Cambridge History of Japan 3: Medieval Japan*. Cambridge University Press, Cambridge, 1990.

Yoshikawa, Eiji. *Taiko*. Kodansha International Limited, Tokyo, 1992.

Zakuragi. "Map of Japan in the 16th Century CE." World History Encyclopedia. 2019.

JOURNALS

'Kansai Window', in *Kippo News*. Vol. 3. No. 91. (June 4, 1996).

Stevens, Carolyn. 'Rocking the Bomb: A Case Study in the Politicization of Popular Culture', in *Japanese Studies* 19:1 (May 1999).

'Tea and the Arts of Japan', in *Chanoyu Quarterly* No. 80 (1995) Urasenke Foundation, Kyoto, Japan.

Travels of Central Japan. Festivals and the Entertainment Arts. The Central Japan Tourism Promotion Liason Council, Nagoya. (Prefectural governments of Toyama, Ishikawa, Fukui, Nagano, Gifu, Shizuoka, Mie, Shiga, Aichi and Nagoya Municipal Government) 1982.

JAPANESE SOURCES

Junior High School History Textbook

資料による新しい歴史
(New History According to Data.)
Hamashima Shoten Publishing Pty Ltd, Nagoya, Japan, 1997 (Pp. 59–73).

Pictorials and Picture Books

Katsumata, Shizuo (text) and Miyashita, Makoto (illustrations)
戦国時代の村の生活
(*Village Life in the Sengoku Era.*)
Iwanami Shoten Publishing, Tokyo, 1988.

Kimura, Shozaburo and Kodama, Kota
内乱から統一へ世界の歴史も分かる日本の歴史ジュニアワイド版
(*From Civil War to Unification, Understanding World History and Japanese History. Junior Wide Series.*)
Vol. 3, Shueisha, Tokyo, 1990.

Reference Books and Chronicles

Aiga, Tetsuo
小学館の学習百科図鑑
(*Shogakkan's Educational Encyclopedia*)
Shogakkan, Tokyo, 1977.

Fujimoto, Atsushi
大阪風の歴史
(*The History of Osaka*)
Yamakawa Publishing, Tokyo, 1969.

Hayashiya, Tatsusaburo
日本の歴史、天下一統
(*Japanese History, Country Unification*)
Vol. 12, Chuokoronsha, Tokyo, 1974.

Inoue M., Kasahara K. and Kodama, K.
詳説日本史
(*A Detailed Explanation of Japanese History*)
Yamakawa Shuppansha, Tokyo, 1989.

Itasaka, Gen
日本を創った100人
(100 Japanese You Should Know)
Kodansha International Limited, Tokyo, 1998.

Kusudo, Yoshiaki
豊臣秀吉九十九の謎
(*99 Riddles of Toyotomi Hideyoshi*)
PHP Kenkyusho, Kyoto, 1996.

Naramoto, Tatsuya
戦国武将
(*Sengoku Generals*)
Shufu-to-Seikatsusha, Tokyo, 1992.

Owada, Tetsuo
日本史年表ハンドブック
(*Timeline of Japanese History Handbook*)
PHP Kenkyusho, Kyoto, 1995.

Suzuki, Kenji
歴史への招待
(*An Invitation to History*)
Nippon Hoso Shuppan Kyokai, Tokyo, 1980.

Watanabe, Takeru
日本史変えた人物200人
(*200 People Who Changed Japanese History*)
Shinjinbutsu Oraisha, Tokyo, 1956. (Pp. 178–179).

Yokoto, Kenichi
ようせつ日本史
(*A Rough Introduction to Japanese History*)
Soogensha, Tokyo, 1978.

日本前史
(*Japan Chronicles*)
Kodansha Limited, 1991.

歴史常識のウソ300
(*300 Lies From Common Sense History*)
Shinjinbutsu Ouraisha, Tokyo, 1991.

NEWSPAPERS, MAGAZINES, GUIDE BOOKS

The Daily Yomiuri Shimbun
Monday September 20, 1997. (p. 13)

Kyoto Shimbun
Sunday April 9, 2000. (p. 1)

本願寺
(*Honganji Temple*)
Honganji Publications Department, Kyoto, 1982.

羽柴秀吉怒涛の天下取り
(*Hashiba Hideyoshi -Taking the Tenka by Storm*)
Gakken, Tokyo, 1987.

大阪城
(*Osaka Castle*)
Osaka Castle Museum, 1990.

秀吉NHK大河ドラマ・ストリー
(*Hideyoshi NHK Taiga Drama Story*)
(Vol. 1) Nippon Hoso Shuppan Kyokai, Tokyo, 1995.

秀吉NHK大河ドラマ・ストリー
(*Hideyoshi NHK Taiga Drama Story*)
(Vol. 2) Nippon Hoso Shuppan Kyokai, Tokyo, 1996.

秀吉と大阪城
(*Hideyoshi and Osaka Castle*)
Osaka City Economic Affairs Bureau, 1988.

ビヅュアル日本の歴史
(Vol. 1. 信長、立つ)
(*Visual Japanese History, Vol. 1-Nobunaga Stands*)
DeAgostini, Tokyo, 2000.

ビヅュアル日本の歴史(Vol. 2. 本能寺、燃ゆ)
(*Visual Japanese History, Vol. 2-Honnoji Burns*)
DeAgostini, Tokyo, 2000.

ビヅュアル日本の歴史
(Vol. 3. 光秀vs秀吉、天下取りの戦い)
(*Visual Japanese History, Vol. 3-Mitsuhide vs Hideyoshi, Battle for the Tenka*)
DeAgostini, Tokyo, 2000.

ビヅュアル日本の歴史
(Vol. 4. 太閤秀吉の誕生)
(*Visual Japanese History, Vol. 4-Taiko Hideyoshi is Born*)
DeAgostini, Tokyo, 2000.

ビヅュアル日本の歴史
(Vol 5. 秀吉の税制改革、検地と刀狩)
(*Visual Japanese History, Vol. 5-Hideyoshi's Tax Reform, Land Survey and Sword Hunt*)
DeAgostini, Tokyo, 2000.

トラベージ (JTBの教育旅行情報誌)
Travage (*JTB Travel Trend and Information*)
(Vol. 16.)
JTB Education and Travel Division, September 1997.

MANGA

織田信長
(*Oda Nobunaga*)
Takahashi Shoten, Tokyo.

Kondo, Ryutaro
織田信長
(*Oda Nobunaga*)
Ginyuusha, Tokyo, 1992.

Kawasaki, Daiji
織田信長
(*Oda Nobunaga*)
Kaiseisha, Tokyo, 1974.

Ooki, Yuuji
豊臣秀吉
(*Toyotomi Hideyoshi*)
Kaiseisha, Tokyo, 1957.

Higuchi, Kiyoyuki
豊臣秀吉
(*Toyotomi Hideyoshi*)
Gakushu Kenkyusha,
Tokyo, 1979.

Higuchi, Kiyoyuki
日本の歴史
(History of Japan)
Gakushu Kenkyusha, Tokyo, 1982.

FILM

Paul Wiegard and Tim Anderson produced:
Kurosawa. A Documentary.
Madman Entertainment Pty Ltd., 2000.
Running Time: 90 mins.

Edward Zwick directed: ***The Last Samurai.***
Warner Home Video Inc., 2003. Running Time: 144 mins.
(Starring: Tom Cruise, Ken Watanabe, Tony Goldwyn, Koyuki, Timothy Spall, Hiroyuki Sanada, Billy Connolly.)

Akira Kurosawa directed: ***Seven Samurai.***
Madman Entertainment Pty Ltd., 1954. Running Time: 207 mins.
(Starring: Toshiro Mifune, Takashi Shimura, Yoshio Inaba, Seiji Miyaguchi, Minoru Chiaki, Daisuke Kato, Isao Kimura, Keiko Tsushima.)

ABOUT THE ILLUSTRATOR

Akihiro Fukuda is a graphic designer and illustrator who has established a successful freelance career for over 30 years in Tokyo. He began illustrating feudal warlords in card games and children's books but has now become a popular illustrator of the infamous *Sengoku Jidai* warlords across all medium. He believes that through his illustrations he can introduce the beauty of Japanese samurai arts, such as swords and armor, as well as the spirit of Bushido.

Currently, he lives in Ichikawa City in Chiba Prefecture. His website can be viewed at **sengoku-gallery.com**

織田信長
Oda Nobunaga

徳川家康
Tokugawa Ieyasu

豊臣秀吉
Toyotomi Hideyoshi

ABOUT THE AUTHOR

Katrice Chanhsamone is a Japanese high school teacher and lover of all things Japanese, especially Japanese history and the *Sengoku Jidai*. During her twenties, Katrice lived, worked, and studied in Toyama Prefecture, Japan. She achieved her Honors degree in Asian Studies at Western Sydney University, majoring in Japanese language and Japanese history before completing a Master's degree in secondary teaching. Pursuing her own life course in Bushido, she attained her second-degree black belt in Kyokushin Karate in Japan. Katrice is currently living in Wollongong, Australia, with her husband and two young sons, where she continues to teach and train, as every dedicated *bushi* should.